CUISINE
SPONTANÉE

CUISINE SPONTANÉE

Fredy Girardet

Translated and adapted by
Susan Campbell

MACMILLAN

A mon père et à ma mère

Copyright © Editions Robert Laffont, S.A., Paris, 1982
English translation copyright © Macmillan London Limited, 1985

All rights reserved. No reproduction, copy or transmission of this
publication may be made without written permission. No paragraph
of this publication may be reproduced, copied or transmitted save
with written permission or in accordance with the provisions of the
Copyright Act 1956 (as amended). Any person who does any unauthorised
act in relation to this publication may be liable to criminal
prosecution and civil claims for damages.

First published 1982 by Editions Robert Laffont, S.A., Paris

First published in the United Kingdom 1985 by
MACMILLAN LONDON LIMITED
4 Little Essex Street London WC2R 3LF
and Basingstoke

Associated companies in Auckland, Delhi, Dublin, Gaborone, Hamburg,
Harare, Hong Kong, Johannesburg, Kuala Lumpur, Lagos, Manzini, Melbourne,
Mexico City, Nairobi, New York, Singapore and Tokyo

British Library Cataloguing in Publication Data

Girardet, Fredy
    Cuisine spontanée
    1. Cookery
    I. Title   II. Campbell, Susan   III. La
    cuisine spontanée. *English*
    641.5   TX717

    ISBN 0-333-39916-1

Designed by Robert Updegraff
Typeset by Bookworm Typesetting
Printed in Great Britain by
St. Edmundsbury Press, Bury St. Edmunds, Suffolk

Contents

Introduction

There are two snapshot-sized photographs on the wall above the varnished pine table that serves as a desk in a corner of Fredy Girardet's restaurant kitchen; one is of his father, the other is of the Troisgros brothers. There are no other decorations, embellishments or mementos at all in this kitchen, which is otherwise severely streamlined and furnished with surgical stainless-steel worktops and huge, crystal-clear windows. The windows overlook the streets and back gardens of the small, grey-and-dun-coloured village of Crissier in Switzerland. The village is bisected, almost gutted, by the spaghetti-junctions of a motorway running north to Neufchâtel and then south and west to Lausanne and Geneva respectively. Its outskirts, a mixture of old farmland, orchards and modern trading estates, merge into the suburbs of Lausanne. Girardet's restaurant occupies the whole of the old Hôtel de Ville, or town hall, of Crissier, and it was here, in one of the downstairs rooms, that his father kept a modest family bistro.

Today Père Girardet's son is described by many as the finest chef in Europe, if not in the world. Tables in his restaurant are booked months in advance by the rich and famous. To connoisseurs of food and wine, his name is almost holy — and yet, when his father died leaving Fredy to run the family business, he was (perhaps not surprisingly as he was only just twenty) more interested in football than in food. He had observed the work in the bistro as a boy, gone through a good but uninspiring apprenticeship in Lausanne, and returned to Crissier to help in the kitchen. The knowledge that he was now expected to spend his life cooking and running a business devoted to the serving of food quite simply bored him.

1

In 1968, when he was thirty-two, a local haulage contractor and wine-lover introduced him to Jacques Parent, a Burgundian wine-grower. He in turn introduced Girardet to three of the most renowned chefs in France: Pierre Bocuse, and Jean and Pierre Troisgros. Their style and their cooking was a revelation to Girardet. For the first time he saw the heights to which a chef with aspirations and ambition could rise, and from then on he knew what he wanted to do. He fell in love with cooking after living with it nearly all his life. Maybe his genius had been there all the time, merely lacking a spark of inspiration to set it free; maybe, because he is a genius, the boredom of cooking routine omelettes, grills and *plats du jour* for a simple bistro could be allayed only by striking out into the more exciting realm of *haute cuisine*. Whatever the cause of this *coup de foudre* or sudden conversion, from then on he began to develop his own style, to remodel the restaurant and, as a result of this single-minded attitude, to become more and more widely appreciated.

In 1975 Fredy Girardet was awarded one of the highest honours in the restaurant trade – the Gault-Millau Guide's *Clé d'Or*. By 1977, the last remaining offices had moved out of the top floor of the town hall and the whole building was now the Restaurant de l'Hôtel de Ville. It has a stylish bar upstairs, two soothing but not ostentatious dining rooms seating seventy people downstairs and, behind them, that enormous, superbly equipped kitchen with eighteen chefs at work in it. Girardet has never worked in anyone else's restaurant and rarely leaves his own. One cannot for a moment imagine that he might leave Crissier and set up in a more fashionable spot. He loves his native soil and lives close to his family and friends.

This brief and already legendary biography may help to explain Girardet's character. Indirectly, it may also cast some light on the nature of the recipes in this book. They are partly founded on the traditions in food (fruit, cheese, cream and good wine) that are local to this particular corner of Switzerland – the Vaud – and partly on his own inspirations. Naturally, a visit to the restaurant will provide a first-hand example of how these recipes should be executed, and in many cases the deftness and elegance of Girardet's presentation may well make the home cook's attempts look desperately clumsy and ham-fisted. (If it is any consolation, the chefs use an electric carving-knife to cut their *galantines* without damaging the slices, as the jelly is so soft.)

The authentic Girardet flavour and touch is nevertheless present in every one of these recipes. Although he would be the first to agree that cooking is not an exact science, his recipes are not at all difficult to reproduce at home as long as the following rules are observed. First, the raw materials must be the very best that can be afforded and must be as fresh as possible; it is useless to expect Girardet's standard of cooking if inferior products are used. Second, the instructions in the preparation sections of the recipes must be followed to the letter; if the cook is directed to take the embryo peas out of mangetouts, to skin the cooked broad beans, to render carrots and lemons into millimetre-fine slices, minuscule dice and thread-sized juliennes, he or she must do so. By preparing the food properly in advance the cooking is more than half accounted for. It will also be seen that the recommended dimensions for terrines, moulds, soufflé dishes, cake tins and tart tins are exactly right; although there is always a generous amount of pastry given for lining tart tins, their fillings never fall short or overflow.

It is tempting to use cheap alternatives where the ingredients are expensive, especially when the recipe calls for foie gras, caviare and truffles. These ingredients are expensive either because they are rare or because they are expensive to produce, but they are not included in the repertoire merely because a wealthy restaurant clientele can afford such luxuries; they are there because of the way in which their particular flavours and textures enhance the dish. Cheaper alternatives can be substituted (if there are any) but, as Fredy Girardet would say, 'It won't be the same.'

Finally, I should explain the title of the book. Faced with an hour or more of preparation, making pastry and stocks, peeling, shaping, de-seeding and slicing vegetables or fruit with mathematical precision, filleting, slicing, chopping and boning fiddly little pieces of meat, poultry, fish or game, the home cook may well feel that *La Cuisine Spontanée* is hardly the most appropriate title. But if we refocus our attention on the simple and speedy manner in which those ingredients are cooked, on the brilliance of some of the combinations and contrasts of flavours and textures, on the playful and deliberate reversals of northern and southern cuisines, and on the happy marriage of rustic and sophisticated ingredients, the title then begins to fit.

Although it would be quite wrong to suggest that he creates new dishes simply for the sake of novelty, Fredy Girardet's greatest enemy is boredom. He hates inaction, boring conversation, boring interviews and boring work as much as he hates ill-cooked and boring food. His talent and his reputation lie in his inventiveness; he thinks up new dishes every day. His creations appear to be 'spontaneous' but they are, of course, the result of over thirty years of dedicated practice at the work he loves best, and at the art of keeping his cuisine sparkling, fascinating and lively.

Susan Campbell
London, April 1985

Editor's Notes

Ingredients

Butter

For all the recipes in this book use unsalted butter.

Butter in sauces. There are many sauces in the book in which butter is incorporated with a sauce base at the last minute by whisking (the French term is *monter au beurre*). For this operation, the sauce should be very hot before the butter is added. The butter should be ice-cold and cut into little pieces so that it can be whisked in bit by bit. Work with the pan close to the heat or over a very low heat, otherwise the butter will just melt without incorporating any of the air that makes the finished result so light and delicate, yet rich and creamy.

Butter for roasting poultry and greasing tins or papillotes. In order to apply a thin coat of butter to poultry before roasting, or to tart tins, cake tins, baking sheets and *papillotes*, the butter should be softened just enough to enable you to paint it on with a large pastry brush.

Crayfish and *langoustines*

Fredy Girardet rarely uses crayfish in his restaurant now, as the wild, native breed is almost impossible to find and the imported ones are more dead than alive by the time they reach him. In the British Isles we may be luckier. Native crayfish are still to be found in some of our streams and, although the breed of crayfish raised on our own fish farms is not thought by Girardet to be equal in quality to a native cray, live farmed crayfish are available at the appropriate season (August to October).

Alternatively, live or frozen raw *langoustines* (Dublin Bay prawns) can be used instead of crayfish.

To kill and shell crayfish and *langoustines*, cook them alive in fast-boiling salted water for ½–1½ minutes (depending on size). Drain them and allow them to cool. Remove the head and claws. Bend the tail so that the shell divides easily across the back at the third joint, counting from the head end. Pull the broken shell off the head end first, then pull the rest of the meat out of the tail end of the shell, pushing it with your thumb from under the tail. Neaten up the head end with a sharp knife, then cut a slit under the tail and carefully pull cut the black, thread-like intestine: failure to do so will give the fish a bitter taste.

Foie gras of duck or goose
Although fresh foie gras is available from a few specialist butchers in London (sometimes it is vacuum-packed), it is still not easy to obtain. Most retail shops find that it is too expensive to risk wastage should any be left unsold. One solution for the home cook is to buy raw foie gras from a restaurant with a regular supply. *Mi-cuit*, or lightly cooked, foie gras is sometimes obtainable; it is not flavoured with herbs or truffles and is suitable for any recipe that requires cooked foie gras. Tinned foie gras is also suitable for such recipes, but pâté de foie gras is not, as it consists partly of other meat.

Frogs' legs
Fresh frogs' legs are occasionally found at specialist shops; frozen frogs' legs are supplied by several frozen-food firms. I have found that the recipes using frogs' legs are equally suitable for chicken meat, but this should not be regarded as a substitute – it is just an alternative ingredient.

Herbs
Herbs are used both for flavour and decoration.

In these recipes herbs are always fresh, never dried. Unless they are to be used in a bouquet garni, herbs with stems should be immaculately trimmed so that only the tender and

6

aromatic leaf is used. Where the recipe states that a herb is to be snipped with scissors, you will usually find that it is to be used as a garnish or to show up in the finished dish, in which case it needs to look elegant. This is easier to achieve by snipping with scissors than by chopping with a knife. Where the instructions are for chopping, the herb is usually to be incorporated in a stuffing or sauce.

Lobsters

Live lobsters are killed instantly by dropping them into boiling water. This method of killing them may seem cruel but there is no kinder way. One minute in boiling water will suffice to kill the lobster and the meat will still be raw. Completely cooked lobsters such as you buy at the fishmonger's will not suit these recipes, as the meat must be raw.

Oil

In any recipe where the ingredient is listed simply as 'oil', use peanut oil.

Pigeons

Tame pigeons are reared for the table in America and on the Continent. Not so here, where we have to be content with wild wood pigeons, which are usually smaller and older than the domestic 'squab'. Squabs are from a larger breed of pigeon and they are killed before they are old enough to fly.

Fredy Girardet's recipes call for a 400g *(14 oz)* pigeon. You are unlikely to find a wild one of that size in Britain – use two average-sized wood pigeons instead. They will weigh about 240g *(8 oz)* each.

For the recipe on page 135, in which a pigeon is completely boned out, you may find it difficult to detach the breast-bone from the flesh without splitting the skin. If the bird is young, you can cut through the edge of the breast-bone and leave it in place, but in an older bird this would not be very pleasing. The only solution is to work as carefully as you can and resort to stitching if the skin splits.

Seasoning

The seasoning of meat and fish is always done just before

cooking; this way you can be sure that it has neither been forgotten completely nor done twice. The salt should be fine sea salt and pepper should be freshly ground, black or white.

In Fredy Girardet's kitchen, poultry or game is first seasoned inside and out with salt, then the outside is brushed with softened butter, and finally, to make sure it sticks, the pepper is added.

Mignonnette pepper is black pepper that has not been ground, but crushed. You can do this with a mortar and pestle. You can also fold a few peppercorns in a cloth or between two sheets of paper and pound them with a bottle.

Poivre rose (also known as pink peppercorns or *baies rose*) has a bright pink, detachable shell and a sweet but peppery flavour. It is sold dried and can be ground in a pepper mill. This spice is not a true pepper but the berry of a plant related to poison ivy. Some people are allergic to it, so it should be used with caution.

For many fish dishes Fredy Girardet prefers cayenne pepper to black or white pepper. This should be used with discretion, as it is the same thing as chilli.

All the necessary seasoning should be done during the cooking of the dish so that nothing needs to be added at table. (You will find no pepper or salt on the tables at Fredy Girardet's restaurant.)

Truffles and truffle juice

If fresh black truffles are unobtainable, use only the very best tinned or preserved kind.

Where a recipe requires truffle juice, use the juice from tinned or preserved truffles. Tinned truffle juice is available on the Continent and in America, but it has not yet met with any demand here. Make enquiries at any shop selling good-quality preserved truffles; they may be able to supply you with truffle juice.

Vegetables and garnishes

Almost all the recipes in this section will be found elsewhere in the book, as, like his sauces, the vegetables often form an integral part of Fredy Girardet's dishes. They are grouped together here so that you can cook them either on their own or as an accompaniment to other dishes. The recipes in which they have already appeared are listed along with other ideas for their use under 'Serving'.

New-season onions are less strong than mature onions. Spring onions may be used instead, but you will need two or three to equal one new-season onion in size.

Vinaigrettes

Fredy Girardet varies the proportions and ingredients of his vinaigrettes subtly from dish to dish; sometimes he uses a mild, herb-flavoured white vinegar, sometimes a stronger red one. The vinegar is usually wine vinegar, although occasionally he uses cider vinegar and sometimes lemon juice. He also uses different kinds of oil, making vinaigrettes with walnut oil, peanut oil and olive oil. He varies the proportions of oil to vinegar, and these are not always given, but are left to the cook's own discretion and imagination. Nor are his vinaigrettes always served cold; there are one or two recipes in this book that use warm vinaigrettes to great effect.

White port

The port in all these recipes should be white port, not red, which is altogether too heavy and sweet. Madeira or dry sherry can be substituted (with discretion) for white port.

Batterie de Cuisine

Cassolettes

The 'cassolettes' in which many of Fredy Girardet's dishes are served in his restaurant are literally miniature, silver-plated, low-sided saucepans. They have little lids and vary in size from about 8–12cm (3–5 in). However, any little dishes or bowls of the same size and shape will serve as cassolettes for the home cook. They can be made of china, metal, or even earthenware.

Frying pans

Because so much of the advance preparation in these recipes includes either partial cooking or very fine slicing and chopping, Fredy Girardet's 'finishing', or final cooking, is usually swift and brief. A frying pan is the ideal pan for this kind of cooking, but to be any use at all it must be the right size and capable of conducting the heat quickly and evenly. Cast-iron pans are best, especially those with non-stick surfaces. Thinner non-stick pans are also useful, particularly if the cooking lasts no more than a few seconds, as is often the case. The size of these pans is important; if you are to succeed with sautées, the pan must be large enough for the food to be turned simply by tossing the pan. There are also several recipes in which the food needs to be cooked in one layer. If the pan is too small, divide the food into two batches, or use two pans.

Oven dishes for roasting
Fredy Girardet invariably starts his roasts by browning the meat on top of the stove. To do this you need a heavy iron pan; the traditional thin, tinned roasting pan supplied with a British domestic oven will not do. It is also unsuitable for the subsequent deglazing of roasting juices and sauce-making with which most of these recipes are finished. If you have a heavy cast-iron roasting pan, enamelled or not, that is ideal; so is a gratin dish made of similar material, or an iron *plat aux oeufs*. Even a cast-iron frying pan will do, provided that it fits in the oven.

Sieves
The most useful sieve for this type of cooking is a *chinois* or conical sieve. Because it tapers to a point it is easier to strain sauces or stocks from one pan to another without spillage. To press the juices well, use a *chinois* in conjunction with a ladle that just fits into the pointed end, or a wooden pestle.

Another useful sieve is the *tamis* or drum-shaped sieve. This is good for purées or pulps. Press the purée through the *tamis* with a flat wooden pusher or *champignon*.

Oven temperatures
These appear to be high by comparison with most cookery books. However, cooking times are correspondingly brief. Occasionally it will be clear that a recipe relies on the heat-retaining properties of a restaurant oven. Unless your domestic oven is similarly well insulated, you will have to adapt the temperature a little.

How to Use the Headings in the Recipes

The recipes are divided into sections under the following headings:

Preparation *(Mise en place)*

This lists everything that can be done in advance.

Cooking *(Cuisson)*

This means more than 20 minutes' cooking time is required for the steps that follow.

Finishing *(Finitions)*

This indicates that you need spend only 10 minutes (or less) on the steps that follow before the dish is ready – including last-minute cooking and sauce-making.

Serving *(Présentation)*

This is self-explanatory, but it should be followed carefully, as the way in which a dish is served is important in this kind of cooking.

Soups

Bouillon of Crayfish with Dill and Caviare

Court-bouillon d'écrevisses à l'aneth et au Beluga

The number of crayfish per person depends on the rest of the menu. Serve each guest with six if there are many dishes to follow, and with ten if the menu is short. Keep the heads, claws and shells in the freezer; they can be used to make crayfish butter (see page 250).

For four people

24–40	large live crayfish (see editor's note, page 5)
1	large tomato
2	green cabbage leaves
1	sprig of dill
	zest and juice of 1 lime
300ml *(½ pint)*	vegetable stock (see page 246)
100ml *(scant ¼ pint)*	champagne *or* dry white wine
½ tsp	fresh ginger root, grated
25g *(1 oz)*	unsalted butter
50g *(1¾ oz)*	Beluga caviare
	salt and pepper

Preparation

1   Leave the live crayfish in a large bowl of cold water for at least 1 hour; this will cleanse them. Cover it securely or they will escape and run all over the kitchen.

2   Throw the crayfish into a large pan of fast-boiling salted water. Bring it back to the boil as quickly as possible, then cook the crayfish for 1½ minutes. Remove them with a slotted spoon and when they have cooled a little take off their heads, claws and shells (see editor's note, page 5). Put the crayfish aside and keep them at room temperature.

3 Peel and de-seed the tomato. Cut the flesh into small dice; you will need about 1 heaped tablespoonful.

4 Blanch the cabbage leaves for 5 minutes in boiling salted water. Refresh them in cold water and drain them. Cut out the largest veins, then cut the leaves into 1cm *(⅜ in)* squares; you will need about 1 heaped tablespoon of cabbage 'squares'.

5 Snip the dill leaves with scissors; you will need about 1 heaped teaspoon of snipped dill.

6 Measure out about 1 teaspoon of grated lime zest and 3–4 teaspoons of lime juice.

Finishing

7 Put the vegetable stock into a saucepan. Add the champagne, snipped dill, diced tomato, chopped cabbage, lime juice and grated zest, grated ginger, salt and pepper. Bring to the boil and set the pan aside.

8 Heat the shelled crayfish tails in the bouillon for 1 minute, then remove them with a slotted spoon. Divide the crayfish equally between four soup-plates, arranging them in a star-shaped pattern.

9 Add the butter to the stock, stir and taste for seasoning.

Serving

10 Pour a ladleful of bouillon over each arrangement of crayfish. Garnish the centres with a spoonful of caviare. Serve lukewarm.

Minestrone with Crayfish

Minestrone d'écrevisses

Lovage (used in this recipe to flavour the soup) is a common plant in the Swiss Alps. It belongs to the celery family.

Editor's note – Lovage is not often seen in the shops, but it grows very well in gardens all over the British Isles. If you have none, a pinch of celery salt with some chopped celery leaves will make the best substitute.

For four people

32	live crayfish (see editor's note, page 5)
4	small new carrots
4	small new turnips
2	shallots
2	cloves of garlic
8	large pods of broad beans
20	lovage leaves (see notes above)
	olive oil
200ml *(scant ½ pint)*	crayfish stock (see page 81, steps 2–4, and make twice the amount)
20g *(¾ oz)*	crayfish butter (see page 250)
150g *(5½ oz)*	unsalted butter
600ml *(1 pint)*	vegetable stock (see page 246)
	salt and cayenne

Preparation

1 One hour in advance, cleanse the crayfish (see page 15, step 1).

2 Cook and shell the crayfish (see page 15, step 2). Keep the carcasses and crush them to make the crayfish stock. Set the shelled crayfish aside.

3 Peel the carrots and turnips and slice them into very thin rounds.

4 Peel the shallots and the garlic and chop both very finely.

5 Pod the broad beans. Cook them for 2 minutes in boiling salted water. Drain them and remove their skins.

6 Chop the lovage leaves.

7   Heat a little olive oil in a saucepan and soften half the
    chopped shallot. Add the crayfish stock and the crayfish
    butter. Reduce this mixture over a high heat for 3–4
    minutes, then add 60g *(2¼ oz)* of the unsalted butter and
    let the mixture bubble for 30 seconds, whisking the butter
    in as it melts. Remove the pan from the heat and season
    with salt and a pinch of cayenne. Set aside.

8   Arrange the shelled crayfish on a baking sheet. Season
    them with salt and cayenne and dot them with 30g *(1 oz)*
    butter, in little pats.

Finishing

9   Heat the grill or oven to 200°C/400°F/Gas 6.

10 Soften the rest of the chopped garlic and shallot in a
    saucepan with a little olive oil. Add the carrots and turnips.
    Let them sweat for 30 seconds, then add the vegetable
    stock. Simmer for 5 minutes, then add the rest of the butter.
    Whisk for 1 minute with the pan still on the heat. Finally,
    add the peeled broad beans, the reduction of crayfish stock
    and crayfish butter, and the chopped lovage. Keep the
    mixture hot.

11 Heat the crayfish on their baking sheet for about 2 minutes,
    either in the oven or under the grill.

Serving

12 Serve the minestrone in soup-plates with the crayfish
    arranged in a circlet around the edges.

Potato Soup
with Mussels and Leeks

Parmentière de moules aux poireaux

For four people

1 litre *(2 lb 4 oz or 2 pints)*	small mussels
1	small leek
200g *(7 oz)*	potatoes
1	small shallot
50g *(1¾ oz)*	unsalted butter
200ml *(scant ½ pint)*	dry white wine
	salt, pepper and cayenne

Preparation

1 Wash the leek and remove the dark green part. You will need 50g *(1¾ oz)* of leek in all, of which half should be white and half pale green. Chop it all very finely.

2 Wash the potatoes but do not peel them. Cook them in salted water. When they are cooked, skin them and put them into a food processor, or pass them through a food mill. Weigh out 150g *(5½ oz)*.

3 Scrape the mussels if necessary. Remove their beards and wash them under running water.

4 Peel and chop the shallot.

5 Melt the butter in a fairly large saucepan, add the shallot and let it cook a little without browning, then add the mussels and the white wine. Let the mussels open over a medium heat with the pan covered. Shake the pan from time to time but do not leave it on the heat for longer than is necessary for the mussels to open, or they will toughen. When they are all open, put a sieve over another saucepan and strain the mussel liquor through it. (If the liquor is very sandy, strain it again through a muslin cloth.) Shell the mussels.

Finishing

6 Add 3 tablespoons of cold water to the strained cooking liquid. Place it on the heat and add the chopped leek. Let it cook for no more than 3–4 minutes so that it stays firm.

7 Whisk the measured-out potato purée into the saucepan with the leeks, a little at a time so that the soup is nicely smooth.

8 If the soup seems too thick, add a spoonful or two of water. Throw in the shelled mussels, bring the soup just to boiling point, take it off the heat and adjust the seasoning with salt, pepper and cayenne.

Serving

9 Divide the mussels equally between four soup-plates, then add the soup.

Warm Mussel and Carrot Soup

Soupe tiède de moules aux carottes nouvelles

For four people

750ml *(1 lb 10 oz or 1¼ pints)*	small mussels
500g *(1 lb 2 oz)*	carrots
1	small shallot
1	sprig of dill leaves
80g *(2¾ oz)*	unsalted butter
200ml *(scant ½ pint)*	dry white wine
	salt

Preparation

1 Peel or scrape the carrots and cut them into rounds, unless they are all very small (in which case keep four whole, with their green tops, for garnish).

2 Peel the shallot and chop it finely.

3 Clean the mussels and remove their beards. Wash them under running water.

4 Pick the dill leaves from their main stem and make them into four little bunches.

5 Put all the carrots into a small saucepan. Just cover them with water, and add a pinch of salt. Cook them until they are

tender but still firm – the time this takes will vary with the age, freshness and size of the carrots, but it will not be more than 10 minutes. Drain the carrots and reserve 3 tablespoons of their cooking liquid.

6 Melt 50g *(1¾ oz)* of the butter in a saucepan. Add the chopped shallot and cook it until it softens, but do not let it brown. Add the mussels and the white wine. Cover the pan and let the mussels open over a medium heat, shaking the pan from time to time and taking care not to leave the mussels cooking for longer than necessary, or they will toughen. When the mussels have opened, strain them through a sieve into a saucepan, keeping the liquid you have strained. Shell the mussels and set them aside.

7 Weigh out 400g *(14 oz)* of the cooked carrots. If you have kept four little ones with green topknots for garnish, set them aside; otherwise, cut 100g *(3½ oz)* surplus cooked carrots into little strips and reserve these for garnish.

   Strain the mussel liquor through a muslin if it is at all sandy, then pour it over the 400g *(14 oz)* cooked carrots. Add the 3 reserved tablespoons of the carrots' cooking water. Bring to the boil and cook the carrots for another 5 minutes.

   Finally, add 30g *(1 oz)* of the butter. Let it melt and remove the pan from the heat.

8 Liquidise the carrots and their second cooking liquid, or pass through a fine vegetable mill until the liquid is the consistency of a thick cream.

Finishing

9 Reheat the mussels slowly in the soup. Take it off the heat as soon as it begins to simmer. If the soup and the mussels are to be reheated from stone-cold, add the mussels after the soup has begun to simmer and do not let them cook at all or they will toughen.

Serving

10 Divide the soup between four heated soup-plates. Decorate each plate with either the whole baby carrots or the little strips of carrot.

Vegetable Soup with Little Shellfish

Soupe de légumes aux petits coquillages

For four people

1	leek, green part only
1	small turnip
1	medium carrot
1	medium Savoy cabbage leaf
1	medium tomato
500ml *(1 lb 2 oz or 1 pint)*	small mussels
500ml *(1 lb 2 oz or 1 pint)*	small clams
4	scallops, *noix* or white parts only
1	new-season onion, with stem
½	clove of garlic
3 tbsps	olive oil
100ml *(scant ¼ pint)*	vegetable stock (see page 246)
3 tbsps	dry white wine
40g *(1¼ oz)*	unsalted butter
	salt and pepper

Preparation

1 Wash the vegetables and, if necessary, peel them. Cut the leek, turnip, carrot and cabbage *en paysanne* – that is, into little squares or triangular pieces of about 1cm × 2mm *(⅜ × ¹⁄₁₀ in)*.

2 Skin the tomato. Remove the seeds and cut the flesh into very small dice.

3 Scrape the mussels, remove their beards, and wash the mussels under running water. Do the same with the clams.

4 If the scallops are still in their shells, open them. Remove the *noix* and wash and clean them. Cut each *noit* into three or four slices, then cut each slice into matchstick-sized pieces.

5 Slice the onion and chop the half clove of garlic.

6 Heat a frying pan with 1 tablespoon of olive oil. Throw in the clams and add half the vegetable stock. Remove the clams with a slotted spoon as they open, or they will toughen. Retain the cooking liquid.

7 Put the mussels to open in a covered saucepan with the white wine and the rest of the vegetable stock. Take care not to leave them on the heat for a moment longer than necessary. Place them in a sieve as soon as they open and keep their cooking liquid.

8 Shell the mussels and clams, using an empty half shell to detach them. Set them aside.

9 Strain both the cooking liquids through a muslin if they are at all sandy, then reduce the combined liquids by half by fast boiling. Set aside.

Finishing

10 Heat 2 tablespoons of olive oil in a saucepan. Throw in the sliced onion and the chopped garlic. Let them soften for 1 minute, then add the reduced shellfish liquor. Bring it to the boil and add the *paysanne* of vegetables. Cook them over a high heat, watching to see that they do not over-cook but that they remain firm. Remove the pan from the heat and gradually whisk in the cold, diced butter.

11 Add the chopped tomato and the mussels to the soup. Return it to the heat and bring it quickly to the boil again. Remove it instantly and add the clams and scallop strips. Adjust the seasoning.

Serving

12 Divide the shellfish and soup between four heated soup-plates.

Cream of Parsley Soup
with a Fricassée of Frogs' Legs

Crème de persil frisé à la fricassée de grenouilles

For four people

12	pairs of frogs' legs (see editor's note, page 6)
2	bunches curled parsley
2	small shallots
60g *(2¼ oz)*	unsalted butter
100ml *(scant ¼ pint)*	dry white wine
150ml *(¼ pint)*	vegetable stock (see page 246)
300ml *(½ pint)*	double cream
	plain flour
	peanut oil
	salt and pepper

Preparation

1 Cut the meat from the frogs' legs by running a knife along either side of the bones. Take the meat from the thigh- and shin-bones. Keep the bones.

2 Trim the parsley leaves from the stems. Weigh out and wash 50g *(1¾ oz)*.

3 Peel the shallots and chop them very finely.

4 Melt 25g *(1 oz)* of the butter in a fairly large saucepan. Add the frog bones and half the chopped shallot. Allow them to colour lightly over a gentle heat for 3–5 minutes, crushing the bones with a spatula. Neither the bones nor the shallot should be allowed to brown.

5 Add the wine and vegetable stock to the bones in the saucepan. Bring to the boil and allow to cook briskly for 8–10 minutes. From time to time crush the bones so that they release all their juices.

6 At the same time, cook the parsley in boiling salted water until it is tender; this will take about 5 minutes. Drain it and put it into a saucepan.

7 Collect all the stock by straining it and the bones through a *chinois*, pressing well to crush out all the juices. Pour the stock over the cooked parsley.

8   Add the cream, keeping aside 1 teaspoonful for the final cooking of the frogs' legs. Bring the soup to the boil, take it off the heat and liquidise it.

9   Pass the soup through a fine sieve once again and set it aside until you are ready for the finishing touches.

Finishing

10 Put the soup into a saucepan. Add salt, pepper and 10g *(¼ oz)* of the butter. Bring to the boil.

11 Season the frog meat with salt and pepper, moisten it with a dash of cream, sprinkle with flour and mix until the meat seems to be coated in sticky cream.

12 Meanwhile, heat a dry, heavy frying pan. Pour a drop of oil into it, add the frogs' legs and stir vigorously with a spatula to separate the pieces.

13 As soon as the meat begins to brown, add the rest of the chopped shallot and 25g *(1 oz)* of the butter. Continue cooking briskly until everything is well browned.

Serving

14 Put two small ladlesful of soup into each plate and pile the frogs' legs in the middle.

Cream of Asparagus Soup with Morels

Crème d'asperges vertes aux morilles

I like to serve a light little soup at the start of a meal. In a menu of four or five courses, this is one of the best soups for sharpening the appetite.

For four people

8	thin green asparagus spears
6	fat green asparagus spears, about 10cm *(4 in)* long
1	medium-sized shallot
100g *(3½ oz)*	fresh morels *or* 15g *(½ oz)* dried ones
100g *(3½ oz)*	unsalted butter
200ml *(scant ½ pint)*	double cream
	salt, pepper and cayenne

Preparation

1 Clean the asparagus spears and cook the thin ones for about 5 minutes and the fat ones for about 10 minutes in boiling salted water. Drain both kinds and reserve the water in which they cooked. Cut off the tips of the eight thin spears and set them aside for the garnish.

2 Peel and chop the shallot finely.

3 Wash the morels carefully and cut them into quarters. (If you are using dried ones, soak them in water for at least half an hour before this step.)

4 Heat half the butter in a saucepan. Add two-thirds of the chopped shallot and colour in the butter. Add the six fat asparagus spears and 200ml *(a scant ½ pint)* of their reserved cooking water. Bring to the boil.

5 Add the cream and reduce it by boiling fast for 2 minutes. Liquidise the soup with 30g *(1 oz)* of the remaining butter. Wash out the saucepan.

6 Strain the liquidised soup through a fine *chinois* or sieve. Season with salt, pepper and cayenne, and return it to the cleaned saucepan. Set it aside.

Finishing

7 Reheat the thin asparagus tips by warming them through in a little of their cooking liquid.

8 Reheat the asparagus soup.

9 Put the morels, the rest of the chopped shallot and the remaining 20g *(¾ oz)* butter into a small saucepan. Season with a little salt and cook gently. The morels will exude a little liquid. Leave them to cook until they have given off all their liquid, at which stage they will be done. Take them off the heat.

Serving

10 Put a ladleful of the soup into each soup-plate. Garnish the centre of each one with a share of morels and two asparagus tips.

Cream of Tomato Soup with Basil
Crème de tomates au basilic

This is an ideal recipe for the end of summer or the beginning of autumn, when tomatoes are at their best.

For four people

600g *(1 lb 5 oz)*	fine ripe tomatoes
6	thin slices of stale French bread
2	large cloves of garlic
1	small new-season onion, with stem
8	basil leaves
½	bay leaf
2	cloves
300ml *(½ pint)*	double cream
20g *(¾ oz)*	unsalted butter
	salt and pepper

Preparation

1 Peel the tomatoes by making a crosswise surface incision in the bottom of each one. Plunge them into boiling water for 30 seconds and remove the skins.

2 Take 2 tomatoes for the garnish. De-seed them and cut their flesh into small dice. Set them aside.

3 Liquidise the rest of the tomatoes and strain the resulting juice. You will need 250ml *(a scant ½ pint)*.

4 Rub the slices of stale bread with one of the garlic cloves, cut in two. Cut the bread into very small cubes and make croûtons by putting them to dry in a low oven.

5 Wash and trim the onion. Peel the second clove of garlic.

6 Snip the basil leaves into small pieces, using scissors.

7 Pour the measured tomato juice into a saucepan. Add the 'aromatics' – the bay leaf, cloves, peeled clove of garlic and onion. Bring the soup to the boil, then lower the heat and let it reduce gently by about half; in an open pan this will take about 10 minutes. Remove the aromatics.

Finishing

8 Add the cream to the soup. Bring it to the boil, whipping it with a whisk as it heats up. Season with salt and pepper. Remove the pan from the heat and, still whipping, add the butter. Emulsify the soup by putting it into the liquidiser. Warm the garlic croûtons.

9 Return the soup to the saucepan. Add the garnish of diced raw tomato and the snipped basil leaves. Bring it to the boil once more.

Serving

10 Serve the soup accompanied by the little garlic croûtons.

Cream of Wild Mushroom Soup with Chervil

Crème de champignons des bois aux pluches de cerfeuil

Ceps *(Boletus edulis)* are not essential for this soup. You could equally well use white field mushrooms *(Agaricus campestris)*.

For four people

200g *(7 oz)*	ceps *or* field mushrooms
1	small shallot
1	very small clove of garlic
2–3	large sprigs of chervil
1 tbsp	oil
20g *(¾ oz)*	unsalted butter
300ml *(½ pint)*	double cream
	lemon juice
	salt, pepper and cayenne

Preparation

1 Clean the mushrooms, throwing away the earthy parts of their stems. Slice very finely.

2 Peel the shallot and clove of garlic and chop very finely.

3 Wash the chervil. Take each leaf off the main stem and arrange the leaves in four little bunches.

4 Heat a heavy iron frying pan. Add the tablespoon of oil. Add the sliced mushrooms and let them colour in the pan over a fairly high heat.

5 When the mushrooms begin to exude their juices, add the butter, chopped shallot and chopped garlic. Add salt and pepper. Stir well and continue to cook the mushrooms until they are well coloured. Remove the pan from the heat and set half the contents aside for the garnish.

6 Pour the cream over the mushrooms that remain in the pan. Scrape the pan well to loosen the sediment and solidified mushroom juices and transfer everything to a saucepan.

7 Boil the contents of the saucepan for 2 minutes, then remove it from the heat. Liquidise the soup.

Finishing

8 Heat the soup in a saucepan and thin it with 1–2 spoonsful of water. Season with salt and cayenne and add a few drops of lemon juice. Bring it to the boil and keep it warm.

9 Reheat the mushrooms for the garnish in a hot oven for a few minutes.

Serving

10 Divide the soup between four heated soup-plates. Put a spoonful of the sautéed mushrooms in the centre of each plate and scatter the bunches of chervil leaves on top.

Terrines

Terrine of Freshwater Fish with Chives

Terrine de poissons du Léman à la ciboulette

Editor's note – As an alternative to dace you could use freshwater trout, or pike, but the trout must have white rather than pink flesh.

For eight to ten people

Mousseline of dace

250g *(9 oz)*	fillets of dace or trout or pike
1	egg white
250ml *(scant ½ pint)*	double cream
	juice of 1 lime
	salt, pepper and cayenne

Rest of the terrine

200g *(7 oz)*	fillets of perch
200g *(7 oz)*	fillets of salmon trout
3	limes
100g *(3½ oz)*	chives
	salt, pepper and cayenne

Preparation

1 To make the mousseline: at least 1½ hours in advance of step 10, put the raw fillets of dace, trout or pike into a food processor or liquidiser with the egg white. Process until you have a very fine purée. Leave the purée to cool for half an hour in the refrigerator.

2 Put the purée into a china or metal bowl and stand it in a large bowl filled with ice-cubes. Make the mousseline by incorporating the cream little by little, beating it in with a

wooden spatula. Taste it, and adjust the seasoning if necessary. Season well with lime juice, salt, pepper and cayenne. Cover the mousseline with transparent film and leave it in the refrigerator for 1 hour.

3   To prepare the rest of the terrine: half an hour in advance of step 10, cut one of the three limes into very fine slices and remove the pips. Line a terrine 30cm *(12 in)* long with the slices of lime.

4   Leave the fillets of perch whole but cut the fillets of salmon trout into strips 1.5cm *(⅞ in)* wide. Squeeze the juice from the two remaining limes and marinate all the fish fillets in it for half an hour.

5   Chop the chives very finely.

6   The terrine is already lined with the slices of lime and the mousseline has been chilled for 1 hour. The fillets of perch and salmon trout have been marinated for half an hour. Now begin to assemble the terrine by making the marinated perch fillets into little rolls, but leave the salmon trout fillets as they are.

7   Cover the lime slices in the terrine with a layer of mousseline 3cm *(1¼ in)* deep.

8   Next, add a layer of rolled perch fillets. Lay them lengthways (not crossways) in the terrine with strips of salmon trout between them.

9   Cover the fillets with a layer of chives and repeat the layers of mousseline, fillets and chives, filling the terrine and finishing with a layer of mousseline.

Cooking

10 Cook the terrine in a bain-marie in a warm oven, 160°C–180°C/300°F–350°F/Gas 2–4, for three-quarters of an hour. Let it cool before unmoulding it.

Serving

11 Serve this terrine with a mayonnaise lightened by a little *crème Chantilly* and scented with chives.

Terrine of Foie Gras of Duck
Terrine de foie gras de canard

Personally, I prefer duck foie gras to goose foie gras. This terrine will keep for about a week in the refrigerator.

For six to eight people

500g *(1 lb 2 oz)* raw duck foie gras (see editor's note, page 6)
Madeira
sugar
salt and white pepper

Preparation

1   Fourteen hours in advance of step 4, put the foie gras to soak for 2 hours in water that is not too cold.

2   Twelve hours in advance, separate the lobes. Slit each lobe lengthways and carefully remove the threads or 'nerves' lying along the inner sides of each lobe. Put the lobes into a soup-plate. Season with 1½ teaspoons of salt and ¼ teaspoon of ground white pepper. Sprinkle with ½ teaspoon of sugar. Finish with a dash of Madeira. Turn the lobes several times to spread the seasoning. Put them in an oval terrine which fits them exactly, cover with transparent film or aluminium foil and leave in the refrigerator for about 12 hours. Allow to return to room temperature before cooking.

Cooking

3   Pre-heat the oven for half an hour to 120°C/230°F/Gas ½.

4   Make a bain-marie by placing folded newspaper in a roasting pan. Stand the terrine on the newspaper. Fill the roasting pan with cold water up to two-thirds of the height of the terrine. Put it in the oven.

5   Turn off the oven and leave the terrine in it for 35 minutes. The fat should be just beginning to run from the foie gras, but it should still be pink inside. (If it is not yet cooked, relight the oven and leave the foie gras to cook until the fat does begin to run.)

6   Take the roasting pan out of the oven and cool the terrine rapidly by holding it under running cold water.

7 Find a little dish or piece of board that fits the shape of the terrine exactly. Cover the foie gras with greaseproof paper, then put the dish or board on top, with a weight on it to press it down lightly. Remove the board before the fat begins to set so that it can cover the whole liver.

Serving

8 Serve the foie gras in its terrine. Using a knife dipped in hot water, cut it into slices about 1cm (⅜ in) thick. Eat the foie gras with toasted brioche.

Jellied Chicken

Gelée de poulette

For twelve people

1	chicken, weighing 1.7kg (3¾ lb)
	softened unsalted butter, to roast the chicken
2	sprigs of tarragon
3 tbsps	mild white wine vinegar
3	fennel bulbs
500ml (1 pint)	chicken aspic (see page 249)
250g (8½ oz)	cooked duck foie gras (see editor's note, page 6)
	oil and vinegar, for a light vinaigrette
	salt and pepper

Preparation and cooking

1 Make this terrine at least 13 hours in advance. Pre-heat the oven to 200°C/400°F/Gas 6. Season the bird inside and out, and brush it with a little softened butter, then roast it in the usual way – that is, for 18 minutes on either side and 9 minutes on its back (45 minutes in all). The meat should be pink.

2 Cut up the chicken, removing all the skin and bones but keeping the meat in whole pieces as much as possible. Bone the thighs and wings as well. Put all the meat on to an oval dish and season it with salt and pepper.

3   Roughly chop the tarragon leaves. Sprinkle a good pinch over the chicken meat.

4   Sprinkle the meat with the vinegar and leave it to marinate at room temperature for at least 1 hour.

5   Reserve one fennel bulb for the garnish and cook the remaining two in boiling salted water until they are tender. Drain them and let them cool, then cut them into slices a good 1cm (⅜ in) thick.

6   Gently heat the chicken aspic until it melts. Stir the rest of the chopped tarragon into it.

7   Cut the foie gras into slices 5mm (³⁄₁₆ in) thick and remove the fat from the edges.

8   To assemble the terrine, 12 hours in advance, pour 5mm (³⁄₁₆ in) of the aspic into the bottom of a terrine measuring 10 × 30cm (4 × 12 in). Put it to set hard in a cool place.

9   Put pieces of chicken on the firm jelly in an even layer, cutting up any pieces that are too large. Follow this with a layer of slices of foie gras, then a layer of slices of fennel, then another layer of foie gras, and finally the rest of the chicken pieces.

10 Fill the terrine with the remaining aspic, topping up the dish to the surface.

11 Leave the terrine, covered with transparent film or aluminium foil, in the refrigerator for at least 12 hours.

Finishing

12 Slice the remaining raw fennel bulb into very fine rounds. Dress them with 3–4 tablespoons of a light vinaigrette, made with mild wine vinegar and not too much oil. Cut the terrine into quite thick slices, taking care not to break them.

Serving

13 Serve one slice of terrine per person, with a few rounds of dressed raw fennel encircling each slice for decoration.

Terrine of Spring Vegetables with Foie Gras

Terrine de primeurs au foie gras

The dish for this terrine should be long and narrow; this makes slicing easier.

For eight to ten people

500g *(1 lb 2 oz)* carrots
500g *(1 lb 2 oz)* turnips
1kg *(2¼ lb)* broccoli
300g *(10½ oz)* parsley
500g *(1 lb 2 oz)* raw duck foie gras (see editor's note, page 6)
100g *(3½ oz)* cooked chicken meat
300ml *(½ pint)* double cream
         sugar
         unsalted butter, softened
         salt and pepper

Vinaigrette
walnut oil
white wine vinegar
salt and pepper

Preparation

1 Make this terrine one day in advance. Peel the carrots and turnips, and cut them into 5mm *(³⁄₁₆ in)* dice. Keep the carrots separate from the turnips.

2 Cut the thickest stems off the broccoli and separate it into little florets.

3 Take the stems off the parsley and weigh out 200g *(7 oz)*. If there is not enough parsley you can add a little broccoli to make up the weight.

4 Soak the foie gras for at least half an hour in tepid water. Separate the lobes and remove the threads or 'nerves'. Put the lobes into a dish and season with salt, pepper and a pinch of sugar.

5 Brush some softened butter round the inside of a terrine measuring 10 × 30cm *(4 × 12 in)*, then line it completely with aluminium foil, the shiny side against the butter. Brush

the matt, inner side of the foil with more butter. Put the prepared terrine in the refrigerator.

6   Cook the parsley for 5 minutes in boiling salted water. Refresh it in cold water, then leave it standing in cold water for about 10 minutes before squeezing it dry in your hands.

7   Cook the carrots for 5 minutes in boiling salted water, then refresh them in cold water and drain them.

8   Cook the turnips for 2 minutes in boiling salted water. Refresh them in cold water and drain.

9   Cook the broccoli for 4 minutes in boiling salted water, refresh and drain.

10 Spread the cooked carrots, turnips and broccoli on a clean cloth and pat them dry.

11 Put the parsley and cooked chicken into a food processor and work the machine until you have a very fine purée. Pass the purée through a *tamis* or drum sieve. It is important to have it very smooth. Cool it for half an hour in the refrigerator.

12 Season the purée with plenty of salt and a very generous grinding of pepper. Put it into a china or metal bowl and stand it in a larger bowl filled with ice-cubes. Make a mousseline by incorporating the cream little by little, beating it in with a wooden spatula. Taste and adjust the seasoning if necessary.

13 Take the prepared terrine from the refrigerator and spread a thin layer of the chicken-and-parsley mousseline over the bottom.

14 Season all the cooked and dried vegetables and mix them into the rest of the mousseline. Half fill the terrine, spreading the mixture with the spatula.

15 Slice the foie gras thickly. Arrange the slices as regularly as possible in the terrine to a depth of about 2cm *(¾ in)*.

16 Finish by filling the terrine with the mousseline. Let it stand at least 1cm *(⅜ in)* above the rim as it will settle when it cooks.

Cooking

17 Pre-heat the oven to 160°C/320°F/Gas 2½–3. Put buttered greaseproof paper over the terrine. Stand it in a bain-marie of cold water and cook for 35–40 minutes. Test to see if the terrine is done by inserting a trussing needle – it should come out dry. Leave the terrine in the refrigerator for at least one night.

Serving

18 Unmould the terrine by giving the bottom a quick dip in hot water. Arrange one or two fairly thin slices on each plate, dressed with a spoonful or two of walnut-oil vinaigrette and garnished with a few leaves of whichever salad is in season.

Salads

Salad of Frogs' Legs
with Fresh Broad Beans

Salade de cuisses de grenouilles aux fèves
fraîches

The number of frogs' legs per person will vary between nine and twelve, according to whether the dish is to be the only *entrée*. They are boned to make them easier to eat.

For four people

2kg *(4½ lb)*	fresh broad beans
18–24	pairs of frogs' legs (see editor's note, page 6)
80g *(2¾ oz)*	thin rashers of smoked bacon
1	medium-sized shallot
1	clove of garlic
3–4	sprigs of flat parsley
1	onion
	plain flour
1 tsp	double cream
	oil
30g *(1 oz)*	unsalted butter
	red wine vinegar
	salt and pepper

Preparation

1 Pod the beans and cook them for 2 minutes in boiling salted water. Drain them and let them cool, then remove the skins.

2 Bone the frogs' legs (see page 24, step 1).

3 Trim the rind off the bacon and cut the rashers into strips 2mm *(⅛ in)* thick.

4   Peel and finely chop the shallot and the clove of garlic.

5   Wash the parsley. Pick the leaves off the stems and chop enough to fill a level tablespoon.

6   Peel the onion and slice it into very thin strips.

Finishing

7   Fry the bacon strips. Drain them on kitchen paper.

8   Put the boned frogs' legs into a soup-plate. Season them with salt and pepper and mix them well. Sprinkle them with a good pinch of flour, then add the cream. Mix by hand; the frogs' legs should be coated in a kind of sticky cream.

9   Put a splash of oil into a non-stick pan and heat it well. Throw in the frogs' legs and stir with a spatula; they will separate from one another easily.

10 When the frogs' legs begin to brown, add the garlic, the shallot and the butter. Continue cooking over a high heat, and when everything is well fried add the parsley, give a stir and remove the pan from the heat.

11 Put the cooked beans, cooked bacon and onions all together in a large bowl. Mix well and season with a vinaigrette made with salt, pepper, a dash of red wine vinegar and a dash of peanut oil.

Serving

12 Arrange the salad of beans in a coronet on each of four plates. Pile a quarter of the frogs' legs in the centre of each coronet. Serve immediately.

Asparagus with Hot Foie Gras and a Warm Vinaigrette

Asperges au foie chaud en vinaigrette

For two people

12	medium-sized asparagus spears
60g *(2¼ oz)*	raw duck foie gras in a slice 1.5cm *(¾ in)* thick (see editor's note, page 6)
1	small shallot
1	sprig of parsley
	seasoned flour
3 tbsps	red wine vinegar
3 tbsps	walnut oil
	salt and pepper

Preparation

1 Trim the asparagus so that each spear is only 10cm *(4 in)* long. Scrape the lower ends if necessary.

2 Peel the shallot and chop it finely.

3 Chop the parsley finely.

4 Lightly dust the foie gras with seasoned flour.

Finishing

5 Cook the asparagus in boiling salted water for 10 minutes. Set the pan aside and keep the spears warm in their cooking liquid.

6 Prepare the warm vinaigrette by cooking the vinegar with the shallot in a little saucepan for 1 minute. Add the walnut oil, season, remove the pan from the heat and keep it warm.

7 Make a non-stick pan very hot, then, without any fat, quickly sauté the slice of foie gras, giving it 40 seconds on each side. Take it out of the pan and cut it into thin slices 3mm *(⅛ in)* thick.

8   Quickly drain the asparagus spears, which you have kept hot. Cut a slice 1cm *(⅜ in)* thick off the end of each stem and add these slices to the vinaigrette.

Serving

9   Arrange the asparagus in a fan shape on two heated plates, with a strip of foie gras on either side of each tip. Spoon the warm vinaigrette over each 'fan' and sprinkle with parsley.

Spring Salad of Quail with Duck Foie Gras

Salade printanière de caille au foie de canard

For four people

2	quails
200g *(7 oz)*	raw duck foie gras (see editor's note, page 6)
100g *(3½ oz)*	dandelion leaves *(pissenlit) or* other salad in season
1	new-season onion, with stem
1	tomato
1	sprig *each* of parsley and thyme *or* other seasonable fresh herbs
	oil
50g *(1¾ oz)*	unsalted butter
	walnut oil
	red wine vinegar
	plain flour
	salt and pepper

Preparation

1   Cut up the quails, raw, in the same way as you would divide a chicken. First cut through the wings at the joint that corresponds to the elbow. Split the breast down the middle, following the breast-bone. Remove both breast fillets, leaving each remaining upper wing-bone attached to each of the fillets. Detach the legs at the hip joints. Cut through the knee joints. You now have four thighs, four drumsticks, and four breast fillets still attached to the upper wing-bone. (Use the discarded parts for stock.)

2   Cut the raw foie gras into 1cm *(⅜ in)* cubes.

3   Clean, wash and dry the salad.

4   Slice the onion finely and cover it to keep out the air.

5   Peel the tomato and halve it across. Scoop out the seeds and cut the flesh into 5mm *(³⁄₁₆ in)* dice.

6   Chop the parsley and other green herbs.

Finishing and serving

7   Sprinkle the pieces of quail with salt and pepper.

8   Make a dry non-stick pan very hot. Add a drop of oil, then, over a brisk heat, cook the pieces of quail, skin-side down to begin with, and almost dry. Turn the pieces after 1 minute. After another minute, add the butter. Reduce the heat to medium and continue cooking for 4 minutes, turning the pieces of quail from time to time.

9   Meanwhile, put the salad into a salad bowl. Make a vinaigrette with salt, pepper, walnut oil and wine vinegar. Season the salad with some of the vinaigrette. Add the sliced onion and mix well. Divide the salad between four plates.

10 When the pieces of quail are cooked, remove the skins. Slice each breast fillet so that it forms a fan, still attached to the wing-bone as if it were a handle. Pass all the quail pieces quickly through the rest of the vinaigrette and arrange them prettily on top of the salad.

11 Quickly roll the cubes of foie gras in flour, then season them with salt and pepper. Sauté them without fat for 40 seconds in a very hot non-stick pan to extract as much fat as possible and to make them very crisp. Take them out with a slotted spoon, pass them quickly through the vinaigrette and arrange them attractively on the salad plates.

12 Dress the tomato dice with the vinaigrette, scatter them over the salad and sprinkle each plate with the chopped herbs. Serve at once.

Salad of Sweetbreads and Mangetout Peas

Salade de ris de veau aux pois gourmands

On no account blanch the sweetbreads!

For four people

2   lobes of veal sweetbreads, each weighing about 250g *(9 oz)*
48 mangetout peapods about 250g *(9 oz)*
1   lime
    walnut oil
    wine vinegar
    olive oil
    salt and pepper

Preparation

1 Soak the sweetbreads for 3–4 hours under running cold water.

2 Using a vegetable knife, peel off the outer membrane and all the fibrous parts. Cut the sweetbreads into slices 5mm *(³⁄₁₆ in)* thick. You should have at least twelve slices.

3 String the peapods. Split them and take out the tiny peas. Cook the pods for 2 minutes in boiling salted water, then drain them.

4 Grate 4 pinches of the zest from the lime and set it aside. Squeeze the juice from the lime and set it aside.

5 Make a vinaigrette with the wine vinegar, walnut oil, salt and pepper.

Finishing

6 Season the cooked mangetouts with the vinaigrette.

7 Season the slices of sweetbread with salt and pepper.

8 Heat a dry non-stick pan. When it is very hot add a dash of olive oil. Add the slices of sweetbread. Let them take a golden colour, giving them 1 minute's cooking on each side. Set them aside on a heated dish and keep them warm while you deglaze the pan with half the lime juice.

Serving

9 Arrange some of the mangetouts in a sunburst pattern on each plate, heaping the rest in the middles. Lay three or four slices of sweetbread on top. Lightly pour the deglazed juices over them and sprinkle them with the grated lime zest and the rest of the lime juice.

Salad of Little Artichokes with Hot Foie Gras

Foie gras de canard chaud en salade

For four people

8	very small purple artichokes
4	slices of raw duck foie gras, each weighing about 50g (1¾ oz) (see editor's note, page 6)
1	onion, peeled and sliced
	unsalted butter
2 tbsps	dry white wine
1	small handful of rocket
	mustard
	oil and vinegar
	plain flour
	salt and pepper

Preparation

1 Trim the artichokes, removing the outer leaves and dry stems if necessary. Cook the artichokes in a pan of boiling salted water to which you have added the sliced onion, the wine and a knob of butter. When they are just tender, drain them and let them cool. Cut each artichoke into eight pieces.

2 Wash and dry the leaves of rocket.

3 Make about 3 tablespoons of ordinary vinaigrette with the mustard, vinegar, oil, salt and pepper.

4 Lightly coat each slice of foie gras with seasoned flour.

Finishing and serving

5 Give the artichoke sections a quick turn in the vinaigrette, then arrange them in a star shape on four small plates.

6 Dress the rocket with the vinaigrette and put a few leaves in the centre of each plate.

7 Heat a dry non-stick frying pan and when it is very hot indeed cook the slices of foie gras, giving them about 20 seconds on each side. Arrange the foie gras slices on the salad and serve immediately.

Warm Asparagus Salad with a Truffle Vinaigrette

Salade tiède de pointes d'asperges sauvages à la vinaigrette de truffes

For this salad I use the slender, wild green asparagus; it is not to be confused with the cultivated kind.

Editor's note – The asparagus sold in England as 'sprue' is the nearest equivalent to wild asparagus, which has a pleasant, slightly bitter flavour, as well as being very slender.

For two people

30	stems of wild asparagus *or* sprue
30g *(1 oz)*	truffles, fresh or tinned (see editor's note, page 8)
2 tbsps	mild white wine vinegar
1 tsp	red wine vinegar
1 tbsp	peanut oil
1 tbsp	walnut oil
2 tbsps	truffle juice (see editor's note, page 8)
1	egg
	salt and pepper

Preparation

1 There is no need to scrape the asparagus, as you will need only the tips. Shorten the stems, therefore, to 5–6cm *(2–2½ in)* and cook them in boiling salted water for about 5 minutes. Drain them but do not let them become cold, as they are to be served warm.

2 In a small saucepan put together the two sorts of wine vinegar, two sorts of oil, truffle juice, salt and pepper: this is the vinaigrette.

3 Hard-boil the egg. Plunge it into cold water, peel it, and chop it coarsely.

4 Chop the truffles very coarsely.

5 Add the chopped egg and chopped truffle to the vinaigrette.

Finishing

6 Warm, but do not cook, the vinaigrette in the little saucepan.

7 If necessary, warm up the asparagus by plunging it briefly into boiling water, then drain it.

Serving

8 Arrange the asparagus in two little bundles on each plate and cover them with the vinaigrette, sharing out the truffles evenly.

Hot Entrées

Asparagus with an Oyster Sauce

Asperges à la mousseline d'huîtres

This recipe combines two different flavours that blend surprisingly well.

For two people

12	medium-sized asparagus spears
4	large oysters
2 tbsps	oyster juice
2 tbsps	dry white wine
2	egg yolks
4 tbsps	asparagus cooking water
1 tbsp	double cream
20g *(¾ oz)*	unsalted butter
	salt, pepper and cayenne

Preparation

1 Shorten the asparagus spears to 10cm *(4 in)* and peel if necessary.

2 Cook them in boiling salted water for 12 minutes. Keep them hot in their cooking water.

3 Open the oysters and retain their juice. Take them out of their shells and trim them. Cut them lengthways into strips 4mm *(⅛ in)* thick.

4 Put the oyster juice and white wine into a small saucepan and reduce by two-thirds.

Finishing

5 To the reduced oyster juice and white wine add the egg yolks, asparagus liquor and cream. Put it over a very low heat and whisk until the sauce becomes a light, thick cream.

6 Season with salt, pepper and cayenne, then, still whisking, gradually add the cold, diced butter.

7 Add the strips of oyster to the sauce and leave it in a warm place at the side of the stove.

8 Drain the asparagus spears. Cut two rounds 5mm (³⁄₁₆ in) thick from the end of each stem and add them to the sauce.

Serving

9 Serve six stems of asparagus on each plate, arranged in a fan shape, with the points dressed in the oyster sauce.

Rabbit Titbits with Morels and Black Truffles

Béatilles de lapin aux morilles et truffes noires

If you want to serve this dish as a main course, double the quantities. You can also make it with veal offal. Use 60g *(2¼ oz)* veal kidney and 60g *(2¼ oz)* calf's liver in place of the rabbit kidneys and liver.

For four people

2	large rabbit livers
2	rabbit kidneys
120g *(4 oz)*	morels
40g *(1¼ oz)*	truffles (see editor's note, page 8)
1	shallot
½	new-season onion
100g *(3½ oz)*	unsalted butter
2 tbsps	Madeira
2 tbsps	white port (see editor's note, page 9)
2 tbsps	truffle juice (optional; see editor's note, page 8)
	oil
1 tbsp	snipped parsley, for garnish
	salt and pepper

Preparation

1 Slice the livers and kidneys finely (about 3mm *(⅛ in)* thick).

2 Carefully wash the morels and cut them in two lengthways.

3 Without peeling them, cut the truffles into 2mm *(1/16 in)* slices.

4 Chop the shallot very finely. You will need 1 heaped teaspoonful. Cut the onion into thin rounds.

Finishing

5 Put 30g *(1 oz)* of the butter into a little saucepan. Add the sliced truffles and the chopped shallot. Put the pan over a high heat. Bring it to sizzling point twice (stirring in between), then deglaze with the Madeira, port and truffle juice. Bring it to the boil again, then add salt and pepper. Keep it warm. This is the base for the truffle sauce.

6 Heat another 30g *(1 oz)* butter in a small pan. Add the morels, leave them to sweat over a fairly high heat until the juices that will run from them during cooking have evaporated. Season with salt and pepper and scatter a pinch of the sliced onion over them. Set the pan aside.

7 Season the sliced livers and kidneys. Put a frying pan over a high heat. Add a splash of oil. Sauté the liver and kidneys in the pan for 20 seconds, add 20g *(¾ oz)* butter, cook for another 20 seconds, then set the pan aside.

8 Finish the truffle sauce by adding 20g *(¾ oz)* butter to the truffles over a brisk heat. Incorporate the butter by shaking the pan as the butter melts. Quickly add the morels.

Serving

9 Serve this dish in four little cassolettes. First spoon out equal amounts of the truffles and morels, then add equal amounts of the rabbit titbits. Scatter a pinch of snipped parsley over each helping.

Pastry Cases Filled with Rabbit Livers and Leeks

Feuilleté au foie de lapin et aux poireaux

A *papet*, or *potée*, of leeks is very much a dish of the Vaudois. Typically, the leeks are cut into larger pieces than they are in the recipe given here, and are cooked with the addition of potatoes. In this recipe, the leeks are cooked in the same way but for a shorter time, as they are more finely sliced and there are no potatoes.

For two people

1	large rabbit liver
1	leek
3 tbsps	double cream
100g *(3½ oz)*	flaky pastry (see page 253) *or* 2 ready-cooked *feuilletés*, each measuring 8.5 × 7cm *(3¼ × 2¾ in)*
1	egg yolk, for glazing
50g *(1¾ oz)*	unsalted butter
	salt and pepper

Preparation and cooking

1 To make the *feuilletés*, pre-heat the oven to 240°C/475°F/ Gas 9. Roll out the pastry and cut two rectangles 8.5 × 7cm *(3¼ × 2¾ in)*. Lightly score through the tops to mark out the lids. Decorate them with a criss-cross pattern and glaze with a little beaten egg yolk. Bake for 20 minutes in the pre-heated oven. Allow them to cool and dry on a rack, then carefully slice the lids off the tops of the *feuilletés*. Even more carefully, scoop out a box-shaped hollow inside each case.

2 Cut the rabbit liver into strips 2cm *(¾ in)* wide and 5mm *(⅛ in)* thick. Season with salt and pepper.

3 Keep only the white and palest green parts of the leek. Strip off the outer leaves, trim the root and cut the leek lengthways into four, then cut it into 1cm *(⅜ in)* pieces. Separate them.

Finishing

4 Reheat the *feuilletés* in a low oven.

5 Put 15g *(½ oz)* of the butter in a small saucepan and soften over a brisk heat. Add 3 tablespoons of water, lower the heat and cook the leeks gently until the liquid has completely evaporated. Add the cream and increase the heat. Cook for 1 minute, season, and remove the pan from the heat. Add another 15g *(½ oz)* butter and keep the leeks warm.

6 Make a frying pan very hot, without adding any fat. Add 20g *(¾ oz)* butter and, just before it starts to colour, add the sliced liver. Cook briskly for 15 seconds, taste and adjust the seasoning if necessary, then put the livers on to a warmed plate.

Serving

7 Put a little of the leek into each of the warmed pastry cases. Divide the rabbit liver between them and cover with the rest of the leek. Put the lids back on to the pastry cases and warm them through again, this time in a hot oven for a few minutes, before serving.

Pastry Cases Filled with Rabbit and Basil

Feuilleté au lapin et basilic

For four people

1	thigh of rabbit, weighing about 350g *(12 oz)*
500g *(1 lb 2 oz)*	broad beans, in their pods
12	leaves of fresh basil
1	shallot
200g *(7 oz)*	flaky pastry (see page 253) or 4 ready-cooked flaky-pastry cases, each measuring 8.5 × 7cm *(3¼ × 2¾ in)*
30g *(1 oz)*	unsalted butter
200ml *(scant ½ pint)*	double cream
	salt and pepper

Preparation

1 If you have not made the pastry cases in advance, roll out the dough and cut four rectangles 8.5 × 7cm *(3¼ × 2¾ in)*, then bake them (see page 58, step 1).

2 Bone the rabbit thigh, removing the skin from the meat. Slice the meat into strips 2cm × 5mm *(¾ × ³⁄₁₆ in)*. You should have 200g *(7 oz)* meat.

3 Pod the beans and weigh out 100g *(3½ oz)*. Boil them in salted water for 2 minutes, then drain them. Peel off the skins and set the beans aside.

4 Chop the basil leaves finely, using a knife.

5 Peel the shallot and chop it.

Finishing

6 Put the lids and cases of the *feuilletés* into a medium oven to re-heat.

7 Put the rabbit strips on to a plate. Crumble them with your hands and season them with salt and pepper. Melt the butter gently in a frying pan. As soon as it starts to foam, add the rabbit meat and the shallot. Stir over a moderate heat for 1½ minutes and, as soon as the meat becomes white all over, remove it from the pan to a plate and keep it warm.

8 Pour the cream into the frying pan. Increase the heat and let it reduce for 2 minutes, then add the basil, salt, pepper and the cooked beans. Allow the mixture to bubble up two or three times, stirring between each time, until the beans are well warmed through.

9 Take the warmed pastry cases from the oven. Using a slotted spoon, transfer a quarter of the beans into each case. Divide the rabbit meat between them. Put the lids on to the pastries and warm them up again, this time for about 1 minute in a hot oven.

10 Add the juices that have run from the cooked rabbit to the sauce. Adjust the seasoning and if it is too thick add a drop or two of water.

Serving

11 Serve one pastry on each plate with a little of the sauce spooned round it and the rest of the sauce in a sauceboat.

Slices of Duck Foie Gras with a Warm Vinaigrette

Escalope de foie gras de canard à la vinaigrette

I serve foie gras with vinaigrette because I do not like rich sauces with it.
Allow 50g *(1¾ oz)* foie gras per person.

For eight people

1	raw duck foie gras, weighing about 400g *(14 oz)* (see editor's note, page 6)
	plain flour
2	shallots
	a small bunch of chives, parsley and chervil
5 tbsps	white wine vinegar
5 tbsps	walnut oil
	salt and pepper

Preparation

1 Separate the lobes of the foie gras and take out the threads or 'nerves'. Cut the foie gras into slices on the slant, 15mm *(½ in)* thick. Try to make eight equal-sized pieces, so that there is one slice for each person.

2 Season each slice with salt and pepper and flour them lightly.

3 Peel the shallots and chop them finely. Measure out 2 level tablespoons of chopped shallot.

4 Chop the herbs finely. Mix them and measure out 2 level tablespoons of chopped herbs.

Finishing

5 Heat a non-stick frying pan.

6 To make the vinaigrette, cook the measured-out shallots in the vinegar, with salt and pepper, for 1 minute. Add the walnut oil, remove the pan from the heat and keep it warm.

7 To cook the foie gras, heat another non-stick pan, without any fat. Quickly fry the slices of foie gras, giving each side 40 seconds. Take the pan off the heat and sprinkle the foie gras with the chopped herbs.

Serving

8 Serve immediately, giving one slice of foie gras to each person with a spoonful of the vinaigrette over it. Serve the foie gras either in little individual cassolettes or on small heated plates.

Little Ravioli with Truffles

Petites ravioles aux truffes

Leftover trimmings from the ravioli dough can be cut into strips or triangles and cooked without delay. Serve them as you would any fresh pasta – with butter and grated cheese, for example.

If this is to be a main course, make double the quantity.

For four people

150g *(5½ oz)*	ravioli dough (see page 253)
25g *(1 oz)*	fresh truffles (see editor's note, page 8)
70g *(2½ oz)*	parsley, weighed without its thickest stems
½	shallot
70g *(2½ oz)*	unsalted butter
1	egg yolk
4 tbsps	truffle juice (see editor's note, page 8)
	salt and pepper

Preparation

1 Make the ravioli dough and leave it to rest for half an hour in the refrigerator, wrapped in plastic or transparent film.

2 Chop up the truffles.

3 Throw the parsley into boiling salted water. Let it return to the boil and cook it for 1 minute, then drain it and refresh it in cold water. Squeeze it well in your hands to press out all the water. When it is well squeezed, chop it finely with a knife.

4 Chop the half shallot finely.

5 To make the ravioli filling, put the chopped shallot into a small saucepan with 20g *(¾ oz)* butter. Put the pan over a brisk heat and remove it as soon as the butter foams. Add the chopped truffles, salt and pepper and put the pan back on a low heat. Leave it to simmer, uncovered, for 2 minutes, stirring all the time. Once again, take the pan off the heat. Add the parsley and mix well. Adjust the seasoning with salt and pepper (after tasting a pinch of the parsley). Put the filling on to a plate and let it cool before you use it. Set aside the pan with its cooking juices.

6 To fill the ravioli, roll out the dough as thinly as you can: it should be almost transparent. The best way to achieve this is to use a little hand-operated pasta machine, working the rollers until you have the thinnest possible sheet of dough in one long piece.

7 Cut the sheet of dough in half. Beat the egg yolk and brush it all over one of the half-sheets of dough. Place the filling in little heaps upon it. There should be sixteen little heaps, each one consisting of about 1 level teaspoon, and they should be at regular intervals.

8 Cover the first sheet with the second sheet of dough. Stick the two layers together by pressing with your fingertips round each of the mounds of filling. Start in the centre to make sure you press out all the air.

9 Using a round pastry cutter or ravioli press of 5cm *(2 in)* diameter, cut out the sixteen raviolis. (The leftover pieces can be used to make a separate dish – see note above.)

Finishing

10 Poach the raviolis for 3 minutes in boiling salted water but do not refresh them in cold water when they are done; instead, drain them and sprinkle them with 20g *(¾ oz)* melted butter. Keep them warm.

11 Put the saucepan in which you cooked the truffles back on to the heat. Add the truffle juice, bring it to the boil, add 30g *(1 oz)* butter and emulsify it by shaking the pan with a circular motion. Adjust the seasoning.

Serving

12 Serve on heated plates, covered with the sauce. Give four or eight raviolis to each person, according to whether this is a first course or a main course.

Asparagus and Fresh Truffles in Flaky Pastry

Dartois aux asperges et truffes fraîches

This is a classic recipe. It should be eaten in good healthy portions as the only *entrée* in a classic menu.

Let the truffles give their scent to the eggs by putting them all together in a closed jar the day before you need them. It is worth the trouble!

For six people

120g *(4 oz)*	fresh cleaned truffles (see editor's note, page 8)
30	stems of green asparagus
3	eggs
1	medium-sized shallot
40g *(1 ¼ oz)*	unsalted butter
800g *(1 ¾ lb)*	flaky pastry (see page 253)
2	egg yolks, for glazing
	plain flour
3 tbsps	white port (see editor's note, page 9)
3 tbsps	truffle juice (see editor's note, page 8)
	a little meat gravy (optional)
	salt and pepper

Preparation and cooking

1 Brush and wash the truffles. Dry them and cut them into slices about 2mm *(¹⁄₁₆ in)* thick.

2 Shorten the asparagus spears to about 8cm *(3 in)* and scrape them if necessary. Cook them in boiling salted water, keeping them firm. Drain them.

3 Hard-boil the eggs. Cool them in cold water, shell them and cut them into rounds.

4 Peel the shallot and chop it very finely.

5 Put the shallot into a non-stick frying pan with a knob of the butter. Heat the pan. When the butter has melted, add the slices of truffle. Season them with salt and pepper and cook them for 2 minutes over a brisk heat. Remove from the heat and let the contents cool in the pan.

6 Roll the flaky pastry into two pieces of equal length. Make one 25cm *(10 in)* wide and the other, which will be the covering piece, about 3cm *(1⅜ in)* wider. Carefully prick the surfaces of both all over with a fork. If you are not going to use the pastry at once, put it into the refrigerator in a plastic bag.

7 Pre-heat the oven to 220°C/425°F/Gas 7.

8 Roll the narrower of the two pieces of pastry on to your rolling pin and unroll it on to a baking sheet.

9 Calculate, by eye, a line 10cm *(4 in)* wide lengthways down the centre of the rectangle and along it arrange half the asparagus spears, placing them head to tail in a single layer. Take care to leave a margin of about 7–8cm *(2¾–3 in)* at each end so that you can seal down the cover. Season the asparagus.

10 Arrange a layer of sliced egg on top of the asparagus. Salt it lightly.

11 Reserve about 20g *(¼ oz)* of the truffles for the sauce. Arrange the rest on top of the egg, still taking care to leave the margins clear. Leave the juices from the cooked truffles in the pan and set it aside.

12 Cover the layer of truffles with the rest of the asparagus, again arranged head to tail, and season lightly.

13 Prepare the pastry glaze by lightly beating the 2 egg yolks with a pinch of salt. Using a pastry brush, paint the margin round the filling with the glaze. Lift the pastry cover on to your rolling pin and lower it carefully over the filling. Pat the filling level with the palms of your hands. Press hard all round the borders of the dough with the flat of your hand to join the two edges together.

14 Trim the edges neatly, leaving a border of only 2–3cm *(1–1½ in)* as a frame for the pastry. Cut the corners off diagonally.

15 Take a spoon-handle with a rounded end and dip it into flour, then press it down at intervals of about 3mm *(⅛ in)* all round the pastry edge to give a decoration of semi-circles. To make sure the edges are properly sealed, you not only need to press down on the spoon but also to push it lightly backwards into the dough.

16 Decorate the surface lightly with a knife, tracing a lattice of diagonal lines. Glaze it.

17 Bake the pastry in the pre-heated oven for 30–35 minutes, checking it from time to time.

Finishing

18 Chop up the truffles that have been reserved for the sauce. Heat the juices left in the pan in which you cooked the first lot of truffles. When it is hot, deglaze with the port and reduce by half.

Add the truffle juice and, if you have it, a little meat gravy.

Add the chopped reserved truffles and whisk in the rest of the butter. Put the sauce in a sauceboat.

Serving

19 Bring the whole pastry to the table and serve it in slices. Pass the sauce round with it.

Onion Tart

Tarte à l'oignon

Every time we try to serve a different appetiser to our clients they clamour for the return of the onion tart.

For six to eight people

Pastry

200g *(7 oz)*	plain flour
130g *(4¾ oz)*	unsalted butter, softened
3 tbsps	water
1	egg
	a pinch of salt

Filling

400g *(14 oz)*	onions
30g *(1 oz)*	bacon, cut into thin strips
50g *(1¾ oz)*	unsalted butter
350ml *(just over ½ pint)*	cream
350ml *(just over ½ pint)*	milk
4	eggs
	a pinch of grated nutmeg
1 level tbsp	chopped parsley
	salt and pepper

Preparation

1   Make the pastry in the same way as you would make *pâte brisée*: that is, make the flour into a 'well' on the pastry board, beat the egg and add it, with the butter, salt and a little of the water, to the centre of the well, then work the ingredients into the flour with your fingertips, incorporating more water little by little; whether you have to use all the water or not depends on the quality of the flour.
Press all the dough together into a ball then, finally, work it thoroughly with the heel of your hand, gathering it up with a pastry scraper as you do so until it is soft and pliable. Leave it in the refrigerator to firm up again before you roll it out.

2   Peel the onions. Cut them into fine rings and weigh out 300g *(10½ oz)*.

3   Cook the bacon strips (which need to be *very* finely cut) in the butter. Let them take on a golden colour, then add the sliced onions and leave them to cook gently until they are tender.

4   In a bowl beat together the cream, milk and eggs, adding salt, pepper and nutmeg to taste.

5   When the onions are cooked, add them to the mixture in the bowl and add the chopped parsley.

6   Roll out the dough 2mm *(⅛ in)* thick and use it to line a buttered tart tin 26cm *(10½ in)* in diameter and at least 3cm *(1¼ in)* deep. Cut a disc of aluminium foil of the same diameter as the tin and place it on the pastry. Weight it down with a handful of beans or crusts.

Cooking

7   Pre-heat the oven to 150°/300°F/Gas 2. Cook the pastry 'blind' for half an hour. Watch the colouring of the edge and as soon as it starts to turn golden remove the aluminium foil and beans or crusts. Cook the pastry shell until the base is baked but not coloured.

8   Fill the shell with the onion mixture. Put the tart back into the oven. Check that the temperature is still 150°C/300°F/ Gas 2 and keep the oven at or just below this temperature for about 1 hour. Towards the end you could reduce the heat a little, as the tart needs to cook very slowly and the temperature at this point varies from oven to oven. The tart is ready if, when you shake it, the filling appears to be quite firm with no hint of a wobble in the centre.

Serving

9   Serve warm, in very small slices as an appetiser, or in larger slices as a first course.

Fish

Fillet of John Dory
with a Compote of Onions

*Aiguillette de Saint-Pierre au confit d'oignons et au
beurre de tomates*

For four people

1	John Dory, weighing 800g *(1¾ lb)*
300g *(10½ oz)*	onions
3 tbsps	red wine vinegar
300ml *(½ pint)*	good red wine
40g *(1¼ oz)*	honey
125g *(4½ oz)*	unsalted butter
3	tomatoes
	oil
	salt, pepper and cayenne

Preparation

1 Peel and slice the onions. Put them into a saucepan with the
vinegar and enough red wine to just cover them. Cook
gently on a low heat until all the wine is absorbed; this will
take about half an hour. Then add 250ml *(a scant ½ pint)*
water. Stir to prevent the mixture sticking to the pan and
continue cooking, still over a low heat, for another half an
hour, or until the onions are completely tender.

Add the honey and 25g *(1 oz)* of the butter. Mix well,
season with salt and pepper, and set the mixture aside. This
is the compote of onions.

2 Cut two of the tomatoes into quarters without peeling
them. Liquidise them, seeds and all. Pass the resulting juice
through a fine sieve and heat it in a little pan until it has
reduced by two-thirds. Set it aside.

3   Peel the third tomato. De-seed it and cut the flesh into small dice.

4   Take the fillets from both sides of the John Dory. Divide each one lengthways into two narrower fillets, following the line down the centre, so that you now have four narrow fillets *(aiguillettes)*.

Finishing

5   Reheat the compote of onions. Taste for seasoning. Add a dash of vinegar and set the pan aside, keeping it warm.

6   Reheat the tomato sauce. Thicken it by gradually whisking in 100g *(3½ oz)* cold, diced butter. Season with salt, pepper and cayenne, and add the tomato dice.

7   Season the fillets of John Dory with salt and pepper. Grill them or fry them in a pan with a drop of oil for 3–3½ minutes.

Serving

8   Serve on heated plates – a spoonful of onion compote down the middle, the fillet of John Dory lying on top (skin-side up), and the tomato sauce on either side.

John Dory with Two Sauces

Saint-Pierre aux deux sauces

The two sauces provide a harmony of contrasts: the sharpness of the red wine against the sweetness of the mousseline.

For four people

1	John Dory, weighing 800g *(1¾ lb)*
2	large shallots
100g *(3½ oz)*	unsalted butter
300ml *(½ pint)*	Brouilly *or* good burgundy
3 tbsps	fish stock (see page 245)
1	sugar lump
100ml *(scant ¼ pint)*	dry white wine
1	small sprig of tarragon
2	egg yolks
3 tbsps	double cream
	oil
	salt, pepper and cayenne

Preparation

1 Peel and chop the shallots.

2 To begin the red wine sauce, soften half the chopped shallot in a saucepan with 15g *(½ oz)* of the butter. Add the red wine and the fish stock. Add the lump of sugar and reduce the liquid until only a quarter of the original quantity is left. Set the reduction aside.

3 To begin the mousseline sauce, put the white wine and the rest of the shallot into a small saucepan and reduce by half. Set it aside.

4 Chop up enough tarragon leaves to fill 2 teaspoons.

5 Cut four fillets from the John Dory.

Finishing

6 Finish the red wine sauce by reheating the reduction, then whisk in 40g *(1¼ oz)* cold, diced butter.

7 Finish the mousseline sauce by adding the egg yolks and cream to the reduction of white wine, whisking them in over a very, very gentle heat (it must be so gentle that you can put your hand on the bottom of the saucepan). When the mixture starts to thicken, gradually add 40g *(1¼ oz)* cold, diced butter, still whisking. Season with salt, pepper and cayenne, and add half the tarragon.

8 Season the fillets of John Dory with salt and pepper. Cook them in a little oil in a very hot non-stick pan, giving each side about 1½ minutes.

Serving

9 Serve each fillet with a little red wine sauce beneath it. Mask them with the mousseline sauce and sprinkle the rest of the chopped tarragon on top.

Fillets of Sea Bass with Artichokes
Escalope de loup aux artichauts

This is a recipe created by my chef, Michel Colin. The cooking time given here is for very large *langoustines*. If you have only little ones it is better simply to heat them in the sauce along with the artichokes and sweet pepper. As soon as they stiffen they can be eaten. You will find that they are ready in a few minutes, without the sauce even reaching boiling point. They can also be cooked in a very hot frying pan for 30 seconds.

For four people

4	pieces of fillet of sea bass, each weighing 70g *(2½ oz)*
4	large *or* 8 small *langoustines* (Dublin Bay prawns)
2	medium-sized violet artichokes
1	small sweet red pepper
6	basil leaves
100ml *(scant ¼ pint)*	double cream
70g *(2½ oz)*	unsalted butter
	dry white wine
	salt and pepper

Preparation

1 Prepare the artichokes (see page 177). Keep 4 tablespoons of their cooking water for the sauce. Cut the artichoke hearts into six sections.

2 Skin the sweet pepper either by dipping it into hot water or, if it is very fresh and firm (as it should be), by peeling it with a potato-peeler. Cut the pepper into julienne strips.

3 Take the shells off the *langoustines* (see editor's note, page 5).

4 Cut the basil leaves finely.

Finishing

5 Put the artichoke water into a small saucepan. Add the cream and reduce by half, then gradually whisk in 50g *(2 oz)* cold, diced butter. Add the artichoke sections and the strips of pepper. Warm them in the sauce but do not let it boil. At the last moment add the basil leaves and adjust the seasoning.

6 Pre-heat the oven to 280°C/530°F/Gas 10. Butter an oven dish with half the remaining butter. Arrange the fillets of sea bass in it and season them with salt and pepper. Add a dash of white wine to moisten the bottom of the dish. Put a little dab of butter on each fillet and place the dish in the oven for 4 minutes, turning the fillets after 3 minutes. Add the *langoustines* after 2 minutes – that is, when the bass is half cooked.

Serving

7 Give each person one fillet on a heated plate, with a garnish of *langoustine* and three sections of artichoke, all covered with the sauce.

Fillets of Sea Bass with Oysters

Escalopes de loup aux huîtres

Editor's note – If the fishmonger opens the oysters for you, make sure he gives you all their juice as well.

For six people

1	sea bass, weighing 1kg *(2¼ lb)*
18	large oysters
100ml *(scant ¼ pint)*	dry white wine
100g *(3½ oz)*	unsalted butter
100ml *(scant ¼ pint)*	double cream
1	sprig of chervil
	salt, pepper and cayenne

Preparation

1   Take the fillets from the sea bass and divide them into six equal-sized pieces. Flatten them slightly by beating them between two sheets of greaseproof paper.

2   Open the oysters, saving their liquid. Set the oysters aside and put the liquid into a small saucepan. Add the white wine and reduce the liquid to a quarter of the original amount.

3   Arrange the pieces of sea bass on a lightly buttered dish. Season them with salt, pepper and cayenne, and sprinkle a few drops of white wine over them.

Finishing

4   Pre-heat the oven to 280°C/530°F/Gas 10.

5   Add the cream to the reduced wine-and-oyster liquid. Bring to the boil and as soon as the mixture emulsifies, thicken the sauce by gradually whisking in the rest of the cold, diced butter. Take the sauce off the stove and adjust the seasoning.

6   Warm the oysters by poaching them for a few moments in the sauce, off the stove. (If the sauce 'falls' a bit after the oysters have been poached in it, take them out, keep them warm and return the sauce to the boil while whisking in a little more butter.)

7 Put the fish fillets into the pre-heated oven for
   2½–3 minutes.

Serving

8 Arrange the fillets of sea bass on six heated plates. Put
   three oysters on each fillet and coat them with the sauce.
   Scatter a few chervil leaves on each helping for decoration.

Fillets of Sea Bass
with Celeriac and Vinegar

Suprême de loup au céleri-rave et au vinaigre

You must be careful not to overdo the vinegar in this dish or you will
spoil the subtle flavour of the sea bass.

For four people

4	fillets of sea bass, each weighing 100g *(3½ oz)*, taken from a fish weighing about 800g *(1¾ lb)*
2	shallots
1	small tomato
2–3	sprigs of chervil
2–3	sprigs of parsley
3 tbsps	red wine vinegar
4 tbsps	white port (see editor's note, page 9)
200g *(7 oz)*	celeriac, peeled
200g *(7 oz)*	unsalted butter
	oil
	dry white wine
	salt and pepper

Preparation

1 Peel and finely chop the shallots.

2 Peel the tomato, after slashing the skin and dipping it for a
   minute or two in boiling water. De-seed it and cut the flesh
   into very small dice.

3 Snip enough chervil and parsley to provide 1 tablespoon of each.

4 Put the chopped shallot and vinegar into a small saucepan and reduce by two-thirds. Add the port. Set aside.

5 Cut the celeriac into little dice 5mm *(³⁄₁₆ in)* square.

Finishing

6 Pre-heat the oven to 200°C/400°F/Gas 6. Using some of the butter, grease an oven dish and arrange the fillets of sea bass on it. Pour a little white wine into the dish. Season the fish with salt and pepper and dot them with a few flakes of butter. Cook in the oven for 2–3 minutes, depending on the thickness of the fish. Turn them over half-way through their cooking. Remove them from the oven, skin them and keep them hot.

7 Heat half a tablespoonful of oil in a frying pan. Throw in the diced celeriac and sauté it briskly over a high heat until it begins to colour. Season, and add a good-sized nut of butter to the pan. Set aside.

8 Reheat the port-and-vinegar reduction. When it comes to the boil, thicken it by gradually whisking in 150g *(5½ oz)* cold, diced butter. Add the diced tomato and the chervil. Taste for seasoning.

Serving

9 Arrange one fillet on each plate with a little heap of celeriac to one side. Cover both fish and celeriac with sauce and sprinkle with parsley.

Brochet of Salmon and Crayfish with Mint

Brochette de saumon et écrevisses à la menthe

For four people

200g *(7 oz)*	salmon, in a slice 1cm *(⅜ in)* thick
16	small live crayfish (see editor's note, page 5)
6	mint leaves
1	carrot
1	onion ⎫ for the mirepoix
1	clove of garlic ⎭
500g *(1 lb 2 oz)*	broad beans, in their pods
	olive oil
	dry white wine
1	sprig of thyme
2	sprigs of parsley
1	sprig of rosemary
100g *(4 oz)*	mangetout peas
60g *(2¼ oz)*	unsalted butter
	salt and pepper

Preparation

1   Cleanse and cook the crayfish (see page 15), giving them 30 seconds' cooking once the water has returned to the boil. Drain them, let them cool a little, then take off their heads and shell the tails (see editor's note, page 5). Crush the shells and set them aside. (Keep the heads and claws for crayfish butter – see page 250.)

2   Roughly chop the vegetables for the mirepoix. Pod the beans. Take the strings off the mangetouts.

3   Put a tablespoon of olive oil into a heavy saucepan. Put it over a high heat and throw in the crushed shells and the mirepoix. Stir while it all cooks, and let the juices evaporate. Add a little white wine: you will need just enough to cover the shells. Add the thyme, parsley and rosemary. Leave to cook gently for 1 hour, watching the level of the liquid from time to time so that finally you are left with at least 100ml *(at least ¼ pint)*. This is the *fond* or stock for the sauce.

4   Pass the *fond* through a sieve. Put exactly 100ml *(a scant ¼ pint)* into a little saucepan. Set it aside.

5 Cut the mint leaves into very fine strips.

6 Cook the beans in boiling salted water for 2 minutes after it returns to the boil. Drain them, skin them and set them aside.

7 Cook the mangetouts in the same way for 2 minutes. Drain them and cut them into squares.

8 Cut the piece of salmon into twenty cubes, each measuring 1 × 1 × 2cm (⅜ × ⅜ × ¾ in). Prepare four brochettes, alternating salmon and crayfish.

Finishing

9 Put the little pan containing the *fond* of crayfish on to the stove. Add 50g (2 oz) cold, diced butter in one go. Whisk it while you bring it to the boil and simmer until the butter and stock are well amalgamated. Pour the sauce into the liquidiser, work the machine for 1 minute, then pour it back into the saucepan and add the mint, beans and little squares of mangetouts. Warm the sauce gently and adjust the seasoning.

10 Cook the brochettes in a non-stick pan with 10g (¼ oz) butter, which hardly needs to melt; 1 minute on each side will be enough for the brochettes, as this is more a matter of heating them than of cooking them.

Serving

11 Divide the sauce and its garnish of vegetables between four plates, putting one brochette in the middle of each.

Paupiettes of Sole and Salmon with Saffron

Paupiettes de sole et saumon au safran

There is no danger of over-cooking the salmon in this recipe because it is rolled up inside the sole which makes it difficult for the heat to penetrate to the centre.

For two people

2	fillets of sole, lightly beaten flat
1	piece of fresh salmon, 2cm *(¾ in)* thick
½	shallot
1	clove of garlic
2	tomatoes
30g *(1 oz)*	unsalted butter
100ml *(scant ¼ pint)*	dry white wine
	a pinch of saffron powder
	a few saffron threads
3 tbsps	cream
1 tbsp	cooked *petit pois* (optional)
	chervil leaves
	salt and pepper

Preparation

1 Cut the piece of salmon into cubes 2cm *(¾ in)* square.

2 Put the fillets of sole on the table, skin-side up. Put half the salmon cubes on to each fillet and roll them up, starting at the widest end. Flatten the *paupiettes* a little by pressing them down lightly, then fasten them with a toothpick.

3 Peel and chop the shallot and the garlic.

4 Peel the tomatoes, de-seed them and cut the flesh into little dice.

Finishing

5 Pre-heat the oven to 220°C/425°F/Gas 7. Use one-third of the butter to grease a little oven dish. Put the *paupiettes* in it with the garlic and shallot. Season with salt and pepper. Add white wine to come up to a third of their height.

6   Cook the *paupiettes* in the pre-heated oven. After 6 minutes, drain off the cooking liquid. Cut each *paupiette* in half, in such a way as to make mini-*paupiettes*. Return them to their dish and put the dish back into the oven. Turn off the oven and leave them for another minute.

7   Meanwhile, add a pinch of powdered saffron and a few threads of whole saffron to the cooking liquid and reduce it by half. Add the cream and the diced tomato. Whisk in the rest of the butter and taste for seasoning. Lastly, add the *petits pois* if you are using them, and simmer for 2 minutes more.

Serving

8   Put two mini-*paupiettes* on each plate. Cover them with sauce and decorate with a few leaves of chervil.

Salmon with Pistou and a Tomato Sauce
Saumon au pistou

If you would like to serve this dish cold in the summer, poach the fish instead of cooking it in the oven.

For four people

2	salmon steaks, 3cm *(¾ in)* thick
36	basil leaves
6	cloves of garlic, inner green parts removed
6 tbsps	olive oil
2	new-season onions, white parts only
4	very ripe tomatoes
15g *(½ oz)*	unsalted butter
1	sprig of fresh thyme
	salt, pepper and cayenne

Preparation

1 To make the *pistou*, put the basil, peeled garlic, olive oil, and some salt and pepper into a liquidiser or food processor. Work the machine until you have a fairly thick purée.

2 To make the sauce, slice the onions, cut the tomatoes into quarters and put them with the onions into a saucepan on the stove. Add 100ml *(scant ¼ pint)* water. Cook until the tomatoes have softened to a pulp, sieve and set it aside.

3 Skin the salmon and bone it. Cut each piece in two horizontally. Arrange the fish in an oven dish smeared with olive oil. (The oven dish needs to be made of a thin metal that conducts heat quickly.) Season with salt, pepper and cayenne, and put a dab of butter on to each piece of fish.

Finishing

4 Pre-heat the oven to 200°C/400°F/Gas 6. Leave the salmon in the oven for 2 minutes, then take it out again. It will continue to cook while you finish the sauces.

5 Reheat the tomato sauce. Season it with salt, pepper, cayenne and fresh thyme. Bring it briefly to the boil.

6 The *pistou* can be eaten hot or cold; to heat it, whisk it while it warms up over a low heat.

Serving

7 Serve each piece of salmon with a little tomato sauce underneath it. Coat with the *pistou*.

Papillote of Salmon with Lime

Saumon en papillote au citron vert

Editor's note – You may find it more economical to make the escalopes from two filleted salmon tails.

For four people

4	escalopes cut from a piece of filleted salmon weighing 800g *(1¾ lb)*
80g *(2¾ oz)*	unsalted butter
	a small piece of fresh ginger root (optional)
1–2	limes
1	large shallot
3 tbsps	white port (see editor's note, page 9)
3 tbsps	double cream
	salt, pepper and cayenne

Preparation

1 Round off the corners of a large sheet of greaseproof paper so that you end up with an oval 60 × 80cm *(24 × 32 in)*. Fold it in half lengthways. Unfold it and butter the centre of one half with 10g *(¼ oz)* butter. Leave the edge that will be folded to close the *papillote* unbuttered, and do not butter the other half, which will cover the fish. (If necessary make two smaller *papillotes*, half the size.)

2 Grate the zest from one lime and squeeze at least 3 tablespoons of juice.

3 Arrange the escalopes of salmon on the buttered half of the *papillote*. Season them with salt and pepper and, if you like, a little freshly grated ginger root. Sprinkle the escalopes with a pinch or two of grated lime zest and a few drops of lime juice.

4 Fold the *papillote* over the fish, making it as air-tight as possible. Press the edges over in small, overlapping folds to make a narrow pleated border. Slide the *papillote* on to a baking sheet and set it aside.

5 Peel and chop the shallot. Soften it in a small saucepan with 20g *(¾ oz)* of the butter. Add 3 tablespoons of lime juice and the same of port. Reduce by half over a brisk heat. Set the pan aside.

Finishing

6 Pre-heat the oven to 280°C/530°F/Gas 10. Cook the *papillote* for 3–4 minutes, depending on the thickness of the escalopes. It will inflate like a balloon.

7 Reheat the reduction of port and lime. Add the cream. Let it bubble once or twice, then thicken the sauce by gradually whisking in 50g *(1¾ oz)* cold, diced butter. Season with salt, pepper, cayenne and, at the last moment, a little freshly grated ginger root and a drop of port.

Serving

8 Bring the *papillote* to the table on a flat dish, with the sauce in a sauceboat. Open the *papillote* in front of your guests. Divide the salmon between the plates and coat each piece with sauce.

Fillet of Red Mullet with Herbs

Filet de rouget aux herbettes

Red mullet is one of my favourite fish; I serve it in fillets simply because my customers are afraid of the bones (see page 89, step 2 if you wish to be extra careful).

Editor's note – Fredy Girardet gives this recipe for one person only. If you are serving more people, increase the quantities accordingly.

For one person

1	fillet of red mullet, taken from a fish weighing about 150g *(5½ oz)*
¼	shallot
¼	clove of garlic
	fresh green herbs (at least four sorts of whichever are in season)
½	tomato
3 tsps	olive oil
5g *(¼ oz)*	unsalted butter
2 tbsps	dry white wine
	salt, pepper and cayenne

Preparation

1   Pre-heat the oven to 280°C/530°F/Gas 10.

2   Peel and chop the shallot and garlic. For one person you
    will need only a pinch of shallot and enough garlic to cover
    the point of a knife.

3   Wash, drain and chop the mixture of herbs; you need
    1 heaped tablespoon per person.

4   Peel the tomato and scoop out the seeds. Cut the flesh into
    small dice; you need 1 level tablespoon per person.

5   Season the red mullet fillet with salt, pepper and cayenne.
    Put the oil and butter into an oven dish that is just big
    enough to take the fish. Lay the seasoned fillet on top.
    Sprinkle it with the shallot and garlic and about
    2 tablespoons of white wine.

Finishing

6   Slide the dish into the bottom of the pre-heated oven. Take
    it out after 2 minutes, turn the fish over and return the dish
    to the oven for 1 minute. Remove the fish from the oven
    and put it on a heated plate to keep it warm.

7   Put the cooking dish over a good heat. Throw in the
    chopped herbs and diced tomato. Bring this sauce to the
    boil, stir it and adjust the seasoning.

Serving

8   Immediately pour the sauce all round the mullet and serve
    at once.

Fillets of Red Mullet with Cream and Rosemary

Filets de rouget à la crème de romarin

I enjoy cooking red mullet with cream precisely because in the places where this fish is found a great deal of olive oil is used.

For four people

4	red mullets, each weighing 150–200g *(5½–7 oz)*
2	medium-sized shallots
50g *(1¾ oz)*	unsalted butter
2	sprigs of fresh rosemary, about 10cm *(4 in)* long
100ml *(scant ¼ pint)*	dry white wine
250ml *(scant ½ pint)*	double cream
	lemon
2 tbsps	olive oil
	salt and pepper

Preparation

1 Scale the mullets and remove the fillets. You can ask the fishmonger to do this, but make sure he gives you the livers and the trimmings, as you will need them too.

2 If you really dislike bones, even the smallest, take out the row of little ones along the inside of the fillets with tweezers. You can find them easily by running an index finger from the head to the tail end.

3 Chop the mullet livers finely.

4 Peel and chop the shallots.

5 Make a *fumet* by melting 30g *(1 oz)* butter in a saucepan. Add the heads and bones of the mullets, broken into pieces, and let them sweat for a few minutes, stirring with a wooden spatula. Add the chopped shallot, stir, let it cook for 2 minutes, then add one of the sprigs of rosemary, broken into four pieces. Add the white wine and 100ml *(a scant ¼ pint)* water, leave to cook gently for 5 minutes, then pass the *fumet* through a sieve. Put it back into a saucepan and reduce it by half.

Finishing

6   Reheat the reduced *fumet.* Add the cream and continue to
reduce the sauce until it lightly coats the back of a wooden
spoon. Take the pan off the heat and gradually whisk in the
remaining 20g *(¾ oz)* cold, diced butter. Add the chopped
livers, season with salt and pepper, and add a drop of lemon
juice. Keep the sauce hot.

7   Heat two non-stick pans. Put a spoonful of oil in each one
and then cook two fillets in each pan, skin-side down to
begin with. Season them and turn them over after half a
minute. Season the other sides and cook for another 30
seconds. Take them off the heat.

Serving

8   Ladle the very hot sauce on to four very hot plates. Put one
fillet on each plate and decorate each with a few rosemary
leaves. Serve at once.

Fillets of Sole
with Leeks and a Red Wine Sauce
Matelote de filets de sole aux poireaux

If this dish is to be served as a first course, one fillet of sole and two
langoustines per person will be sufficient.

For four people

8	fillets of sole
8	*langoustines* (Dublin Bay prawns)
400g *(14 oz)*	leeks
1	small shallot
90g *(3¼ oz)*	unsalted butter
150ml *(¼ pint)*	fish stock (see page 245)
300ml *(½ pint)*	Brouilly *or* good burgundy
1	sugar lump
	salt and pepper

Preparation

1 Clean the leeks. Cut off half the green part and cut the rest into 1cm *(⅜ in)* pieces.

2 Peel and chop the shallot finely.

3 Heat 25g *(1 oz)* of the butter in a saucepan. Add the leeks, stir for 1–2 minutes, then add a good 100ml *(a scant ¼ pint)* water. Continue cooking until the moisture has completely evaporated (about 5 minutes). Adjust the seasoning. Add 10g *(¼ oz)* butter and set the pan aside.

4 Sweat the shallot in a saucepan with 15g *(½ oz)* butter. Add 100ml *(a scant ¼ pint)* of the fish stock and all the wine, leaving 3 tablespoons of fish stock in reserve. Add the sugar and let the sauce reduce by three-quarters. Set the pan aside.

5 Take the shells off the *langoustines* (see editor's note, page 5).

6 Use about 10g *(¼ oz)* of the butter to grease an oven dish. Season the fillets of sole and arrange them in the dish. Sprinkle the 3 reserved tablespoons of fish stock over them.

Finishing

7 Pre-heat the oven to 280°C/530°F/Gas 10.

8 Reheat the leeks and the red wine reduction.

9 Cook the fillets of sole in the pre-heated oven for 3 minutes, adding the *langoustines* after 1 minute. Take the dish out of the oven and pour the cooking liquids into the red wine reduction.

10 Quickly make the sauce by whisking in the remaining 40g *(1¼ oz)* butter, cold and diced, over a brisk heat. Taste for seasoning.

Serving

11 Arrange a bed of leeks on each of four heated plates. Put the fish on top of the leeks and coat everything with the red wine sauce.

Ragoût of Monkfish with Saffron

Ragoût de lotte au safran

Monkfish is an interesting fish; personally, I prefer it grilled, baked or fried, rather than poached.

For four people

300g *(10½ oz)*	boned monkfish
150g *(5¼ oz)*	boned salmon
3	cloves of garlic
4	basil leaves
1½ tbsps	olive oil
	saffron powder and threads
3 tbsps	vegetable stock (see page 246)
150ml *(¼ pint)*	double cream
2 tbsps	*petits pois*, cooked
2 tbsps	broad beans, skinned and cooked
	lemon juice
	salt and pepper

Preparation

1 Cut the monkfish so that each person will have three pieces measuring about 4 × 3cm *(1½ × 1³⁄₁₆ in)*.

2 Cut the salmon into cubes a good 1cm *(⅜ in)* square.

3 Peel and chop the garlic very, very finely.

4 Using scissors, cut the basil leaves into very fine strips.

Finishing

5 Put 1 tablespoon of the olive oil into a small saucepan, add the chopped garlic and a pinch of saffron powder and sweat for 3 minutes over a medium heat. Add the vegetable stock, the double cream and a few threads of saffron. Continue cooking at a bare simmer for 2 minutes. Taste for seasoning and add a little lemon juice. Add the *petits pois* and beans and set the pan aside.

6 Make half a tablespoon of olive oil very hot in a non-stick frying pan. Season the monkfish with salt, pepper and saffron powder and sauté it briskly for 3 minutes. Set it aside.

7   Make another, dry, non-stick frying pan very hot. Season the diced salmon in the same way as the monkfish, with salt, pepper and saffron powder. Sauté for 30 seconds, stirring all the time with a spatula. Set it aside.

Serving

8   Put three pieces of monkfish in the centres of four heated plates. Cover them with sauce. Garnish with a few salmon cubes and sprinkle the strips of basil over all.

Grilled Fillets of Dace or Trout with Tarragon

Gratin de féra à l'estragon

Editor's note – For remarks on dace, see editor's note, page 33.

For four people

4	fillets of dace *or* trout, each weighing 80–90g (2¾–3½ oz)
2	sprigs of tarragon
4 tbsps	whipping cream
2	egg yolks
150ml (¼ pint)	double cream
50g (1¾ oz)	unsalted butter
250ml (scant ½ pint)	dry white wine
½	lemon
	salt and pepper

Preparation

1   Pre-heat the oven to 280°C/530°F/Gas 10.

2   Chop enough tarragon leaves to fill 2 teaspoons.

3   Whisk the whipping cream until it thickens.

4   Beat the egg yolks with all but 3 tablespoons of the double cream.

5   Butter an oven dish with 20g (¾ oz) of the butter. Arrange the fillets on it and season them. Add the white wine.

Finishing and serving

6   Slide the dish containing the fish into the pre-heated oven. Leave it there for 1½–2 minutes, or longer, depending on the thickness of the fish. Take it out and remove the skins from the fish. Put the fish into a shallow, heat-proof dish and keep them hot.

7   Pour the liquid that remains in the cooking dish into a saucepan. Add the tarragon and reduce the liquid by about two-thirds. Whisk in 30g *(1 oz)* cold, diced butter and the remaining double cream. Let the sauce reduce for a moment, then pour it, still whisking, on to the egg-yolk-and-cream mixture.

8   Put the sauce back into a saucepan over a very gentle heat and let it thicken, whisking all the time, until it shows signs of boiling. Take it off the stove, and season with salt, pepper and a little lemon juice. Carefully incorporate the whipped cream.

9   Pre-heat the grill. Ladle the sauce over the fish, or, if your dinner plates can stand the heat of a grill, put each fillet on to a plate and coat it with the sauce. Put them under the grill and leave them until the sauce turns golden – this will not take long, only about 1 minute, so watch carefully. Serve at once.

Fillet of Dace
with Lemon, Capers and Tomato

Filet de féra meunière à la brunoise de citron, câpres et tomate

Editor's note – For remarks on dace, see editor's note, page 33.

For four people

4	fillets of dace *or* trout, each weighing 90g *(3 ¼ oz)*
2	lemons
2	large tomatoes
60	capers
1	new-season onion
	chives
1	sprig of parsley
1–2 tsps	cream
	plain flour
1 tbsp	oil
80g *(2¾ oz)*	unsalted butter
	salt and pepper

Preparation

1 Peel the lemons down to the raw flesh and cut them into very small dice of 3mm *(⅛ in)*. Remove all the pips.

2 Peel the tomatoes, de-seed them and cut the flesh into 3mm *(⅛ in)* dice.

3 Roughly chop the capers and slice the onion into fine rounds.

4 Cut the chives finely; you will need 1 teaspoonful.

5 Form the parsley into a neat little bouquet to decorate the serving dish.

6 Brush the cream on to the fish fillets. Flour them, shaking off the excess. Season with salt and pepper.

Finishing

7 Heat the tablespoon of oil in a non-stick frying pan. Put the
   fillets in the pan. Turn them after 1 minute. Add 50g *(1¾ oz)*
   butter and let it foam. Take out the fillets when they are a
   golden colour and keep them warm. Keep the pan hot and
   replace the fish with the chopped onion and capers. Add
   the remaining 30g *(1 oz)* butter and the diced lemons. Cook
   for 1 minute. Add the diced tomato, adjust the seasoning,
   cook for another 30 seconds, then take the pan off the heat.

Serving

8 Arrange the four fillets in a fan shape on a hot serving dish.
   Cover them with the sauce. Sprinkle the chopped chives on
   top and decorate with the little bouquet of parsley.

Shellfish
and Crustaceans

Cassolette of Oysters Girardet

Cassolette de Belons Girardet

Good, flat oysters are essential for this dish or the result is disappointing.

For four people

16	large oysters
1	carrot
1	leek, white part only
1	stick of celery
150ml *(¼ pint)*	champagne
1 tbsp	double cream
100g *(3½ oz)*	unsalted butter
	salt, pepper and cayenne

Preparation

1 Cut the carrot, leek and celery into matchstick-thin julienne strips, 7–8cm *(2¾–3 in)* long. In all, you will need 80g *(2¾ oz)* – that is, 25–30g *(¾–1 oz)* of each vegetable.

2 Open the oysters and save their juices in a little saucepan, or if the fishmonger opens the oysters for you, make sure he gives you their liquor as well.

3 Add the champagne to the oyster juice and reduce until no more than 4 good tablespoons of liquid remain.

Finishing

4 Reheat the reduction of champagne. Add the cream. Bring it to the boil, then thicken the sauce by gradually whisking in 100g *(3½ oz)* cold, diced butter. Season with salt, pepper and cayenne.

5   Put the julienne of vegetables into a colander or wire sieve and dip them into boiling salted water for 1 minute. Drain them.

6   At the same time, warm the oysters in the hot sauce for 30 seconds only.

Serving

7   Put four oysters on to each heated plate. Scatter the julienne of vegetables over them. Coat them with sauce and serve immediately.

Hot Oysters with Courgettes
Huîtres chaudes aux courgettes

Editor's note – This recipe needs skillful last-minute serving. It is therefore easier to make it for only one or two people. To make it for more, increase the ingredients accordingly.

For one person

3	large oysters
1	courgette, about 12cm *(4¾ in)* long
2 tbsps	double cream
65g *(2¼ oz)*	unsalted butter
	lemon juice
	seaweed, for decoration (ask for it when you buy the oysters)
	salt, pepper and cayenne

Preparation

1   If your fishmonger opens the oysters, make sure he also gives you their liquid. If you open them yourself, save the liquid. Put it into a small saucepan. Keep the oyster shells too.

2   Arrange the three lower shells on a large plate or dish covered with a bed of seaweed.

3   Wash and dry the courgette. Slice it very finely; you will need about ten slices, each 2.5mm *(⅛ in)* thick, per oyster.

100

4   Reduce the oyster liquid by two-thirds over a brisk heat. Pass it through a fine sieve lined with muslin to avoid any grit. Wash out the saucepan and put the reduced and strained liquid back into it.

Finishing and serving

5   Bring the reduced oyster liquid to the boil. Add the double cream. Cook it quite fast and let it reduce for 1 minute.

6   Still over a good heat, thicken the sauce by gradually whisking in 50g *(1¾ oz)* cold, diced butter. When all the butter is emulsified, add a drop or two of lemon juice. Remove the pan from the heat and taste for seasoning. Whisk it for a few moments more, off the heat.

7   Heat the remaining 15g *(½ oz)* butter in a non-stick pan and add the courgette slices. Season them with salt, pepper and cayenne. Cook them for just long enough to heat them through, then set them aside.

8   Put the three shelled oysters into the sauce. Heat them in it over a very low heat for 30 seconds, *en vannant* – that is, shaking the pan with a circular movement. Take the oysters out of the sauce and put one in each of the half shells that are waiting on their bed of seaweed.

9   Working very quickly so that nothing is too cold, arrange about ten courgette slices over each oyster in a fish-scale pattern.

10 Reheat the sauce for a moment, whisking it over the heat. Pour it very carefully over each oyster.

11 A simpler, but much less pretty, presentation is to dispense with the shells and seaweed and simply serve the oysters, courgettes and sauce in little individual cassolettes or soup-plates.

Grilled Scallops and Langoustines with Asparagus

Grillade de Saint-Jacques et langoustines aux asperges

Editor's note – The corals of the scallops are not used in this recipe. Keep them for another dish. Well cooked and diced, they can be used as a garnish, incorporated in a sauce, or added to a mousse.

For four people

8	scallops
8	large *langoustines* (Dublin Bay prawns)
12	green asparagus spears
1	lemon
1	sprig of dill
4 tbsps	olive oil
	salt and pepper

Preparation

1 Reduce the asparagus to a length of 10cm *(4 in)*, peeling them if necessary. Cook them in boiling salted water for 10 minutes. Drain them and dry them on a cloth.

2 If you have bought the scallops in their shells, shell them, wash and clean them. Keep only the *noix*.

3 Shell the *langoustines* (see editor's note, page 5).

4 Squeeze the lemon, measuring out 4 tablespoons.

5 Chop the dill and measure out 2 heaped teaspoonsful.

Finishing

6 Put the lemon juice into a little saucepan. Add salt and pepper. Add the olive oil, whisking it in as if you were making a vinaigrette. Put it on to the stove and just warm it through. Add the dill.

7 Reheat the asparagus tips by putting them into a colander or sieve and plunging it into a saucepan of boiling water for 1 minute. Drain them.

8 Season the *langoustines* and scallops with salt and pepper and grill them, giving the *langoustines* 1 minute and the scallops 2. If you have no grill you can cook them both in a very hot non-stick pan with a drop of olive oil.

Serving

9 Arrange three spears of asparagus in a fan shape at the top of each heated plate, put the scallops in the middle and two *langoustines,* in a V-shape, below them. Coat everything with the warm oil-and-lemon sauce.

Mousse of Scallops with Citronnette Sauce
Mousse de Saint-Jacques à la citronnette

This is a very light mousse as there is hardly any egg in it. Serve one or two moulds per person, according to the size of the rest of the meal.

Editor's note – Fredy Girardet's *citronnette* sauce is a lemony version of a vinaigrette.

To fill twelve 5cm- *(2 in-)* diameter moulds

300g *(10½ oz)*	scallop *noix* or whites (about 6 large ones)
6	large scallop corals
1	egg
	a dash of cognac
	a dash of white port (see editor's note, page 9)
450ml *(¾ pint)*	double cream
	unsalted butter, to grease moulds
50g *(1¾ oz)*	caviare
2	lemons
6 tbsps	olive oil
2	sprigs of dill
2	large ripe tomatoes
	salt, pepper and cayenne

Preparation

1 Cook the corals for 5 minutes in a little water. Drain them, then cut them into 5mm *(³⁄₁₆ in)* dice.

2 Put the white muscular parts of the scallops (the *noix*) into a food processor with a pinch of salt and purée them. Add the egg and process again, seasoning with a good pinch each of pepper and cayenne. Add a dash of cognac, the same of port and, still working the processor, add the cream little by little. Adjust the seasoning, which should be quite definite (especially the pepper and cayenne).

3 Stir the diced corals into the mixture.

4 Butter the twelve 5cm- *(2 in-)* diameter moulds.

5 Half fill the moulds with the mousse, then to each one add about ½ teaspoon caviare. Top up the moulds with mousse and rap each one on the table to level the surface. The mousse should not quite reach the top.

6 Squeeze the lemons, measuring out 3 tablespoonsful of juice. Pour it into a small saucepan. Add the 6 tablespoons of olive oil and season with salt and pepper.

7 Snip the dill finely with scissors; you will need 3 tablespoonsful. Peel and de-seed the tomatoes. Cut the flesh into small dice; you will need 3 tablespoonsful. Add the dill and tomato to the seasoned mixture of oil and lemon.

Finishing

8 Pre-heat the oven to 220°C/425°F/Gas 7.

9 Arrange the filled moulds in a roasting pan. Fill it with water to half its depth. Cover the moulds with buttered greaseproof paper and cook them in their bain-marie for 10 minutes in the pre-heated oven.

10 Warm the *citronnette* over a low heat.

Serving

11 Unmould the mousses and serve them (one or two per person) on heated plates surrounded by the *citronnette*.

Papillote of Scallops and Langoustines with Coriander

Papillote de Saint-Jacques et langoustines à la coriandre

For two people

4	large scallops
2	large *or* 4 small *langoustines* (Dublin Bay prawns)
	coriander seed (in a pepper mill)
1	new-season onion, with stem
	a small bunch of chives
70g *(2½ oz)*	unsalted butter
½	tomato
3 tbsps	dry white wine
	salt, pepper and ground or crushed pink pepper *(poivre rose)* (see editor's note, page 7)

Preparation

1 Open the scallops, if they are still in their shells. Clean them under running water. Keep the white muscular parts (the *noix*) and two of the best corals so that you have two *noix* and one coral per person. Cut the *noix* in half horizontally.

2 Shell the *langoustines* (see editor's note, page 5)

3 Season the *noix*, corals and *langoustines* with salt, pepper and a good pinch of *poivre rose*. Give them five or six turns of the pepper mill containing the coriander seeds as well.

4 Cut the onion into thin rounds.

5 Snip the chives with scissors.

6 Heat a nut of the butter in a non-stick pan over a medium heat. Throw in the sliced onion and the chives. Add the scallop *noix*, cooking them for 20 seconds on each side.

Add the *langoustines*, removing them as soon as they stiffen. Add the corals and leave them for 2 minutes, turning them from time to time. Take each of the different ingredients out of the pan as they become ready and set them aside on a plate. Keep the juices in the pan, as you will need them (and it) later on when you make the sauce.

7 Prepare two *papillotes* from two sheets of greaseproof paper measuring 40 × 20cm *(16 × 8 in)*. Fold the papers in half across the longest side and round off the two open corners with scissors. Open the papers again and brush them with softened butter. Arrange the papers so that the 20cm *(8 in)* sides face you. On each of the halves nearest to you arrange four slices of scallop, one coral and one or two *langoustines*. Scoop the flavourings and seasonings from the pan juices and scatter them over the fish.

8 Fold each *papillote* in two again and close the edges firmly, bending them over in small, tightly pressed-down, overlapping folds. They will make a neat border 1cm *(⅜ in)* wide.

9 Peel and de-seed the half tomato. Cut it into 5mm *(³⁄₁₆ in)* dice.

Finishing

10 Pre-heat the oven to 280°C/530°F/Gas 10. Put the *papillotes* on a baking sheet and cook them for 3½ minutes (or a little longer if your oven is not able to reach that very high heat).

11 At the same time, reheat the pan used for the preparatory cooking. Dilute the contents with the wine, scraping the sediment with a spatula. Transfer everything to a small saucepan.

12 Put the saucepan over a medium heat, bring the contents to the boil, simmer for half a minute, then gradually whisk in 40g *(1¼ oz)* of the cold, diced butter, still over a medium heat, until it emulsifies (but the sauce should not be too thick as we are not making a *beurre blanc*). Season to taste with salt, pepper, a pinch of *poivre rose* and a few turns of the coriander mill. Add the diced tomato and a pinch of snipped chives. (The whole procedure for making this sauce takes only 3 minutes.)

Serving

13 Serve the *papillotes* on heated plates with the upper parts cut with scissors into the shape of a lid. Pour a good tablespoonful of sauce into each *papillote*.

Scallops with Chicory and Lime

Saint-Jacques aux endives et citron vert

This is one of my oldest recipes, but the harmony of tastes is still as good as ever.

For four people

8	scallops
400g *(14 oz)*	chicory
1	lime
½	lemon
20g *(¾ oz)*	sugar
120g *(4 oz)*	unsalted butter
	oil
3 tbsps	dry white wine
3 tbsps	white port (see editor's note, page 9)
½ tbsp	double cream
	salt, pepper and cayenne

Preparation

1 Open the scallops, if they are still in their shells. Wash them under running water. Set the whites (the *noix*) and the corals aside.

2 Do not wash the chicory, but wipe and dry it carefully. Cut each *chicon* into small triangular pieces by slicing it diagonally, starting at the tip, and rolling it through a quarter-turn with each slice. Put all the slices into a big bowl and separate them by hand.

3 Remove the zest from the lime as thinly as possible, so as to leave all the pith behind. Cut the zest into long, very fine julienne strips. You will need 2 pinches of julienne.

4 Squeeze the juice from the lime: you should have 2 tablespoonsful. Squeeze the half lemon as well; you need 1 tablespoonful of lemon juice.

Finishing

5 Season the chicory with the 2 tablespoons of lime juice, the sugar, 2 good pinches of salt and several turns of the pepper mill (this also stops it going black). Mix everything together carefully with your hands.

6 Melt 25g *(1 oz)* of the butter in a large, well-heated saucepan. Add the chicory and stir it over a very brisk heat for 2 minutes to bring out its liquid. Add 2 teaspoons of the lemon juice and, still over a brisk heat, continue cooking for 1 minute but no longer, stirring all the time. Set the pan aside.

7 Season the scallops with salt, pepper and cayenne. Heat a non-stick frying pan. Add a drop of oil. When it is really hot, cook the scallops for exactly 1 minute on each side. Set the pan aside.

8 Pour the white wine and port into a small saucepan and let them reduce a little over a high heat. Add the double cream. Let it bubble up twice, then thicken the sauce by gradually whisking in 100g *(3½ oz)* cold, diced butter. Season with salt, pepper and the last drops of lemon juice.

Serving

9 Put a large spoonful of chicory on to each of four heated plates. Lay two *noix* and two scallop corals on each bed of chicory, cover the scallops with a little sauce and scatter a few lime-zest threads on top.

Feuilleté of Scallops with Two Purées

Saint-Jacques en feuilleté aux deux purées

For four people

8	scallops
200g *(7 oz)*	flaky-pastry dough (see page 253) *or* 4 ready-cooked flaky-pastry cases, each measuring 8.5 × 7cm *(3¼ × 2¾ in)*
2	shallots
60g *(2 oz)*	unsalted butter
300ml *(½ pint)*	double cream
	lemon juice
1kg *(2¼ lb)*	*petits pois* in their pods *or* 450g *(1 lb)* shelled *petits pois*
	sugar
1 tbsp	fresh herbs, finely chopped
	salt, pepper and cayenne

Preparation

1   If the pastry cases have not been made in advance, roll out the dough and cut four rectangles 8.5 × 7cm *(3¼ × 2¾ in)*, then bake them (see page 58, step 1).

2   If they are still in their shells, shell the scallops. Wash them well. Set the corals aside. Cut the white *noix* into cubes 1cm *(⅜ in)* square. Set them aside.

3   Peel the shallots and chop them finely. You will need 2 level tablespoonsful.

4   To make the purée of corals, fry the corals whole for a few minutes with a good knob of butter. Add 1 tablespoon of the chopped shallot and continue cooking for 1 minute more. Take the pan off the heat. Reduce the corals to a purée in a food processor or liquidiser, adding 30g *(1 oz)* of the butter and all but 4 generous tablespoons of the cream. Season with salt and pepper.

Put the purée into a small saucepan. Let it reduce and thicken for 2 minutes. Adjust the seasoning if necessary and add a few drops of lemon juice. Set this purée aside.

5 To make the purée of *petits pois*, pod the peas if necessary. Cook them *à l'anglaise* – that is, cook them in boiling salted water, uncovered, for about 10 minutes (if you are using frozen peas they will need only 5 minutes). Drain them. You will need a small teacupful of peas, about 110g *(4 oz)* for each *feuilleté*.

Reduce the peas to a purée, either in a food mill, through a sieve, or through a *tamis*.

Season the purée with salt, pepper and a pinch of sugar. Add the 4 reserved tablespoons of cream and mix well in a saucepan over a gentle heat. Set this purée aside.

Finishing

6 Reheat the *feuilleté* lids and cases in a moderate oven.

7 Reheat both purées over a gentle heat.

8 Season the diced scallop *noix* with salt, pepper and cayenne. Sauté them briskly in a frying pan with 30g *(1 oz)* of the butter, a tablespoon of chopped shallot, and the chopped fresh herbs. Thirty seconds will be long enough, as you need only just warm the scallops.

Serving

9 Put 2 good tablespoons of *petits pois* purée into the bottom of each *feuilleté*, then make a layer of the diced *noix*. Cover this with the coral purée and put the lids on top. Serve them like this or, if you like, add a light anchovy butter – but this is not really necessary.

Lobster Claws
with a Cream of Sweet Peppers

Pinces de homard à la crème de poivrons

This recipe is further proof of how the products of the Mediterranean can do very well without their traditional accompaniment of olive oil.

Editor's note – Although it will not look so elegant, the home cook may find it less wasteful to use a whole lobster for two people rather than run to the expense of using just four pairs of claws.

For two people

8	large uncooked lobster claws *or* 1 large live lobster (see editor's note, page 7)
1	sweet red pepper
	unsalted butter
1 tbsp	olive oil
100ml *(scant ¼ pint)*	double cream
100ml *(scant ¼ pint)*	vegetable stock (see page 246)
	salt, pepper and cayenne

Preparation

1 Blanch the lobster claws in boiling salted water for 3 minutes. If you are using a whole live lobster, kill it by plunging it into boiling salted water for 2–3 minutes.

2 Crack the claws and take out the meat, keeping it intact. If you are using a whole lobster, split the tail down the middle and take out the meat.

3 Arrange the shelled meat on a buttered oven dish. Season with salt, pepper and cayenne.

4 Dip the red pepper into boiling water and peel it. Take out the seeds and cut out the white parts. Cut the flesh into fine julienne strips.

5 Cook the julienne in the olive oil for 3–4 minutes until they are *al dente*. Set them aside in the pan.

Finishing

6 Pre-heat the oven to 200°C/400°F/Gas 6.

111

7   Reheat the pan containing the julienne of pepper. Add the double cream, season and let the mixture reduce over a high heat for about 3 minutes. If need be, dilute it with 1–2 spoonsful of vegetable stock. Set it aside in the pan.

8   Put a knob of butter on each piece of lobster meat and slide the dish into the pre-heated oven. Leave it for 2 minutes, then take it out again; you need only warm the lobster meat, not cook it.

Serving

9   Arrange four claws (or half a lobster) per person on heated plates. Coat the lobster with the sauce.

Cassolette of Lobster with Broad Beans

Cassolette de homard aux fèves fraîches

For two people

1	live lobster, weighing 500g *(1 lb 2 oz)* (see editor's note, page 7)
500g *(1 lb 2 oz)*	broad beans, in their pods
1	leek, white part only
1	clove of garlic
20g *(¾ oz)*	celery
1	new-season onion, with stem
2	tomatoes
1	sprig of thyme
1 tbsp	oil
70g *(2½ oz)*	unsalted butter
3 tbsps	white port (see editor's note, page 9)
10g *(¼ oz)*	black truffle (see editor's note, page 8)
3 tbsps	double cream
	salt, pepper and cayenne

Preparation

1   Pod the beans. Blanch them for 2 minutes in boiling water. Drain them, let them cool a little, then skin them. You will need about 2 heaped tablespoons of cooked, skinned beans.

2   Kill the lobster by plunging it into a large pan of already boiling salted water. Leave it in the boiling water for 1½ minutes, then take it out. It will now be dead, but still quite raw. Let it cool a little, then shell it. Remove the claws and legs first. Shell the tail so that the meat stays intact. Remove the coral, if it has any. Break up the shell. Take the meat out of the claws and legs, using a hammer and a special pick. Keep all the claw meat intact if possible. Collect all the leg meat and set it aside with the claw meat in a buttered gratin dish. Cut the tail in half lengthways, removing the black, thread-like intestine. Put the tail meat into the gratin dish with the other lobster meat.

3   Slice the white part of the leek. Cut the clove of garlic in two, the celery into dice and the onion into rounds. Skin and de-seed the tomato, then cut the flesh into little dice. Strip the leaves from the sprig of thyme.

4   Heat a tablespoon of oil in a sauté pan. Throw in the garlic, celery, onion and thyme. Sweat them for 2 minutes, then add the broken-up carcass of the lobster and continue cooking, stirring and pressing the juices from the various ingredients. After 3–4 minutes, add the diced tomato and 50g *(1¾ oz)* of the butter. Leave the mixture to simmer for 2–3 minutes more over a medium heat before moistening it with the port and 3 tablespoons of water. Let it reduce gently for 10 minutes, still over a medium heat. Remove from the heat and pass it through a sieve, pressing well. Put the resulting sauce back into a saucepan and set it aside.

5   Chop the truffle coarsely.

Finishing

6   Pre-heat the oven to 280°C/530°F/Gas 10.

7 Reheat the sauce. Add salt, pepper, cayenne and the double cream. Simmer gently for 3 minutes. Pass the sauce through a fine *chinois* or sieve and return it to the saucepan.

8 Add the 2 tablespoons of beans and the chopped truffle to the sauce. Leave it to keep just hot enough to warm the beans through without cooking them.

9 Put 2–3 knobs of butter on to the pieces of lobster meat and slide the gratin dish into the oven. Leave it for 2½ minutes, or for as long as it takes to make the lobster very hot.

Serving

10 Divide the lobster equally between two heated plates. Serve with the sauce poured over.

Langoustines, Scallops and Lobster with Black and Pink Pepper

Langoustines, Saint-Jacques et homard aux deux poivres

A large frying pan is recommended for this recipe, but you can also use a medium-hot grill, as long as you take great care with the cooking times.

For two people

1	small live lobster, weighing 400g *(14 oz)* (see editor's note, page 7)
2	scallops
4	*langoustines* (Dublin Bay prawns)
3	large shallots
65g *(2¼ oz)*	unsalted butter
½ tsp	black peppercorns, crushed *(mignonnette)* (see editor's note, page 7)
½ tsp	pink peppercorns, crushed *(poivre rose)* (see editor's note, page 7)
	oil
	salt

Preparation

1 Cook the lobster for 2 minutes in boiling salted water. Take it out of the water, let it cool, then detach the tail and claws. Cut the tail in two lengthways, and take out the meat. Shell the claws, taking care to keep the meat intact.

2 If the scallops are still in their shells, take them out. Wash them under running water and keep the white muscular parts *(noix)*. (Keep the corals for another recipe.)

3 Shell the *langoustines* (see editor's note, page 5).

4 Peel and chop the shallots; you will need 2 heaped tablespoonsful.

5 Put the 2 tablespoons of chopped shallot into a small frying pan with 40g *(1¼ oz)* of the butter, the black pepper, pink pepper and a pinch of salt. Cook until the shallot softens, but do not let it colour. Set the pan aside.

Finishing

6 Heat 1 tablespoon of oil in a large cast-iron pan. Cook the scallop *noix* over a brisk heat for 1½ minutes, then, still with a brisk heat, add the *langoustines.* At this precise moment, turn the scallops over and push them to one side of the pan where they will not cook so fast. Wait 30 seconds, then add the pieces of lobster meat. Place them too on the side of the pan, away from the hotter centre. Wait 1 minute, then add 25g *(1 oz)* of the butter to the pan. Let it froth, then baste the scallops and *langoustines.* Take both out of the pan and keep them hot. Give the lobster a quick basting with the butter, then take it out and keep it hot with the rest.

7 Pour the cooking butter into the pan containing the shallots and pepper, and put it on the stove to reheat.

Serving

8 Cut the scallops in two horizontally. Share out the different shellfish between two heated plates and arrange them as nicely as you can. Taste the sauce for seasoning, then coat each helping with it.

Cabbage-leaf Parcels Stuffed with Langoustines

Petits choux farcis de langoustines au beurre de Beluga

This recipe embodies the rustic and the refined, which is the kind of union I like. The cabbage and the *langoustines* both have a hint of sweetness. The caviare provides the contrast.

For four people

1	Savoy cabbage
16	large *langoustines* (Dublin Bay prawns)
40g *(1 ¼ oz)*	large-grained Beluga caviare
140g *(5 oz)*	unsalted butter
2	medium-sized shallots
100ml *(scant ¼ pint)*	dry white wine
1 tbsp	double cream
	salt, pepper and cayenne

Preparation

1 Choose eight good leaves from the cabbage. Blanch them in boiling salted water for 2–3 minutes until they are tender (give them longer in winter, when the leaves are tougher). Drain them and lay them flat on a cloth.

2 Shell the *langoustines* (see editor's note, page 5). Season them with salt, pepper and cayenne.

3 Heat 20g *(¾ oz)* of the butter in a frying pan over a medium heat. Cook the *langoustines* in it for no more than 1 minute – just long enough for them to stiffen. Take them out.

4 Remove the large central rib from the drained cabbage leaves. Place two *langoustines*, tails crossed, on each leaf. Fold the leaf to make a little parcel. Put the little parcels, pressed together, in a small enamelled cast-iron oven dish. Put a knob of butter on each parcel and leave them in the refrigerator.

5 Peel and finely chop the shallots.

Finishing

6 Pre-heat the oven to 230°C/450°F/Gas 8.

7 To make a reduction for the sauce, cook the chopped shallots with the wine in a small saucepan until the wine has reduced to 2 tablespoons.

8 Heat the stuffed cabbage leaves in the oven for 4–5 minutes.

9 Add the double cream to the reduction of white wine. Bring it to the boil and thicken the sauce by gradually whisking in 100g (3½ oz) cold, diced butter. Season with salt, pepper and cayenne.

Serving

10 Serve each person with two little cabbage-leaf parcels on heated plates. Pour the melted butter from the oven dish into the sauce. Place a teaspoonful of caviare on each parcel, coat with sauce and serve at once.

Poultry
and Rabbit

Chicken Breasts with Leeks and Truffles

Aile de volaille aux poireaux et aux truffes

For two people

2	*suprêmes* (breasts) from a chicken weighing about 1.5kg *(3½ lb)*
2	medium-sized leeks, each weighing about 200g *(7 oz)*
1	small shallot
40g *(1¼ oz)*	truffles (see editor's note, page 8)
300ml *(½ pint)*	chicken stock (see page 243)
1½ tbsps	truffle juice (see editor's note, page 8)
80g *(2¾ oz)*	unsalted butter
3 tbsps	double cream
	salt and pepper

Preparation

1 Take the two *suprêmes* from the chicken in such a way as to include the shoulder joint and upper part of the wing. Cut off the rest of the wing just at the elbow joint. You now have the two breasts, filleted, with each one still attached to its upper wing-bone. Make a pocket in each breast, just where the muscles can be prised apart.

2 Clean the leeks, cutting off half the green and keeping the rest. Cut them into 1cm *(⅜ in)* pieces. You will need 300g *(10½ oz)* in all.

3 Peel the shallot and chop it.

4 Cut half the truffles into slices and the rest into 5mm *(³⁄₁₆ in)* dice.

5   Stuff the *suprêmes* with the slices of truffle. Season inside the openings and close them with toothpicks.

6   Put 100ml *(a scant ¼ pint)* of the chicken stock into a small saucepan with a tablespoon of truffle juice. Heat it and reduce it by about two-thirds, or until there are only 2 tablespoons of liquid left in the pan. Set it aside.

Finishing

7   Season the outsides of the *suprêmes* and poach them gently in 200ml *(a scant ½ pint)* of chicken stock for 8–10 minutes. The meat must stay soft and just pink inside.

8   Melt 30g *(1 oz)* of the butter in a sauté pan. Add the chopped shallot and the leeks. Stir for 1 minute, then add 100ml *(a scant ¼ pint)* water. Cook until all the water has completely evaporated, then add the cream and diced truffle. Season and continue cooking over a brisk heat until the cream coats the leeks nicely. Finish by adding 20g *(¾ oz)* butter and the remaining drops of truffle juice. Taste for seasoning. The leeks should still be slightly crunchy.

9   Reheat the reduction of chicken stock and truffle juice, and gradually whisk in the remaining 30g *(1 oz)* cold, diced butter. Taste for seasoning. Again, the leeks should still be slightly crunchy.

Serving

10 Arrange the leek-and-truffle mixture on heated plates. Put the chicken breasts on top and coat each breast with the sauce.

Chicken Fricassée with Cucumbers and Tomato

Fricassée de volaille aux concombres et à la tomate

For four people

1	farmyard chicken, weighing 1.4kg *(3 lb)*
½	carrot
½	onion
½	white part of a leek
¼	celery stick
1	clove of garlic
1	sprig of thyme
2	cucumbers
1	sprig of parsley
5	chive leaves
1	large ripe tomato
1 tbsp	oil
90g *(3¼ oz)*	unsalted butter
200ml *(scant ½ pint)*	white wine
3 tbsps	white port (see editor's note, page 9)
3 tbsps	Madeira
200ml *(scant ½ pint)*	double cream
	salt and pepper

(carrot, onion, white part of a leek, celery stick, clove of garlic, sprig of thyme — for the mirepoix)

Preparation

1 Cut the chicken into six pieces – two thighs, two drumsticks and two pieces of breast with the top wing joint (see page 46, step 1). Keep the wing tips and the ribcage to help make the sauce, breaking up the bones.

2 Chop all the vegetables for the mirepoix into rough dice.

3 Peel the cucumbers. Cut them into 4cm *(1½ in)* lengths, dividing each piece lengthways into quarters so that you can remove the seeds. Next, trim each piece into the shape of a spindle or elongated clove of garlic.

4 Snip the parsley and chives finely with scissors. Peel the tomato, scoop out its seeds and cut the flesh into small dice.

Cooking and finishing

5 Pre-heat the oven to 280°C/530°F/Gas 10. Choose a roasting pan or gratin dish that is large enough to allow all the chicken pieces and broken bones to lie side by side. Pour in a tablespoon of oil and add the mirepoix of vegetables and the bones. Put the dish on top of the stove over a moderate heat and let everything take colour, turning the bones over as they do so, for 3 minutes.

6 Season the pieces of chicken and lay them side by side, skin-side down. Dot them with 60g *(2¼ oz)* of the butter, cut into pieces, and leave the dish over the heat for 1 minute more. Turn the chicken pieces over and put the dish into the pre-heated oven. After 5 minutes, remove the breasts and keep them hot. Five minutes later, take the dish out of the oven and put all the meat together on a serving dish. Keep it hot.

7 While the chicken is cooking, blanch the cucumber pieces by plunging them into a large pan of boiling salted water. As soon as they begin to look transparent, they are cooked. Take them out and drain them.

8 To make the sauce, put the dish in which the chicken cooked back on to the stove. Deglaze it with the white wine, port and Madeira, scraping the bottom well and pressing the bones to extract all their juices. Allow the gravy to cook for 3 minutes, then strain it into a small saucepan. Let the gravy bubble up twice. Add the cream and continue simmering until the sauce starts to thicken; this will take about 2 minutes.

9 Add the cucumbers to the sauce and let it cook until it just coats the back of a spoon. Gradually whisk in 30g *(1 oz)* cold, diced butter. Season with salt and pepper. Add the diced tomato.

Serving

10 Arrange the chicken pieces on a large dish. Coat them with the sauce, arranging the bits of cucumber and tomato prettily. Scatter the snipped parsley and chives over all.

Braised Chicken with Chicory and Green Peppercorns

Poularde de Bresse braisée aux endives et poivre vert

For four people

1	chicken, weighing 1.4kg *(3¼ lb)* after cleaning and trussing
1kg *(2¼ lb)*	chicory
¼	celery stick ⎱ for the mirepoix
1	carrot ⎰
2	cloves of garlic
1	shallot
1	onion
1–2	lemons
2 tbsps	oil
170g *(6 oz)*	unsalted butter
100ml *(scant ¼ pint)*	white port (see editor's note, page 9)
100ml *(scant ¼ pint)*	chicken stock (see page 243)
15g *(½ oz)*	caster sugar
4 tsps	green peppercorns
	salt and pepper

Preparation

1 Season the chicken inside and out with salt and pepper, then truss it.

2 Make the mirepoix by cutting the carrot and celery into tiny cubes of 2–3mm *(⅛ in)*.

3 Peel the garlic, the shallot and the onion. Cut the shallot in half and the onion into quarters (you will use only one-quarter of the onion).

4 Do not wash the chicory, but wipe it carefully. Remove any limp or damaged outer leaves. Cut them carefully in the following way: hold the end in your left hand and make the first cut, on the slant, about 2cm *(¾ in)* from the end. Give the chicory a quarter-turn and slice again, as before. Continue until all the chicory is sliced into small, triangular pieces. Separate them and set them aside in a salad bowl.

5 Press the juice from the lemons. You may need one or two, depending on their juiciness; you need 4 tablespoons of juice in all.

Cooking and finishing

6 To cook the chicken, pre-heat the oven to 200°C/400°F/ Gas 6. Pour 2 tablespoons of oil into a heavy iron roasting pan. When it is really hot, put the bird into the pan, on its side. Seal and colour it well all over, on a brisk heat, taking in all about 10 minutes. As the bird begins to colour, drain off the oil and replace it with 50g *(1¾ oz)* butter. Add the mirepoix, garlic, quarter onion and halved shallot. Put the pan into the pre-heated oven. Roast the bird for 30–35 minutes, basting it often and turning it to cook on all sides. Leave it on its back for the last 5–10 minutes. Be careful not to burn either the vegetables or the butter.

When the bird is cooked, take it out of the roasting pan and keep it warm. Pour off the cooking fat but leave the vegetables in the pan.

7 To make the sauce, pour any juices that have collected inside the cooked chicken into the roasting pan. Put 20g *(¾ oz)* butter into the roasting pan, heat it on the stove and deglaze with the port. Let the liquid bubble up two or three times, scraping all the sediment and juices from the bottom of the pan. Next, add the chicken stock. Bring the sauce to the boil once more, then strain it into a small saucepan, pressing the vegetables well in the sieve.

8 Finish the sauce by bringing it to the boil again. Add the green peppercorns with 1 tablespoon of the lemon juice, then gradually whisk in 50g *(1¾ oz)* cold, diced butter.

9 To finish the chicory, season the pieces in the salad bowl with the sugar, 3 pinches of salt, 10 turns of the pepper mill and 3 tablespoons of lemon juice. Mix well with your hands. Use two frying pans and heat 25g *(1 oz)* butter in each. Divide the chicory between them and cook briskly for 3 minutes, stirring all the time as the chicory exudes its liquid. Transfer it to a heated serving dish that is also large enough to take the chicken.

Serving

10 Put the chicken on to the heated serving dish with the chicory forming a bed underneath. The chicken can be served whole or cut into four. Give it a light covering of the sauce and serve the rest of the sauce in a sauceboat.

Poached Chicken with a Cream of Watercress Sauce

Poularde pochée à la crème de cresson

The taste of watercress goes very well with chicken. If you like, you can create a very pretty effect by pushing a few watercress leaves under the skin of the chicken breast before you truss the bird.

For four people

1	chicken, cleaned and trussed, weighing about 1.4kg *(3¼ lb)*
150g *(5½ oz)*	watercress leaves (taken from 3–4 bunches), stripped of their stems
100g *(3½ oz)*	unsalted butter
8	small young turnips, round or long, with stems
8	medium-sized young carrots, with stems
12	medium-sized new potatoes
3	medium-sized leeks
2	small celeriacs
	lemon juice
250ml *(4½ pints)*	chicken stock (see page 243)
	bouquet garni (1 leek, 1 onion and 1 carrot)
150ml *(¼ pint)*	double cream
	salt and pepper

Preparation

1 To make the base of the watercress sauce, wash the watercress leaves, dry them thoroughly and put them in a food processor. Work the machine until the leaves have become almost completely liquid. Add the butter, bit by bit, so that the mixture becomes a watercress butter. Let it solidify in the refrigerator while you continue with the rest of the preparation and cooking.

127

2   Wash and prepare all the vegetables: peel the turnips and carrots but leave a little topknot of green stems on each one; peel the potatoes; cut the leeks into 5–6cm *(2–2½ in)* lengths; peel and cut the celeriacs into quarters, trimming them to form shapes similar to large cloves of garlic and sprinkling them with lemon juice to keep them white.

Cooking and finishing

3   Measure the stock into a deep pan which is just large enough to hold the chicken – about 25cm *(9¾ in)* in diameter. Put it on to the stove, add the bouquet garni, salt it lightly and, when it comes to the boil, put the chicken into it. Let it poach for half an hour in barely trembling liquid. Take it off the stove; it will keep hot in its bouillon.

4   Fill four saucepans with salted water and bring them to the boil. Cook the celeriac and turnips together, but cook the carrots, leeks and potatoes in separate pans. Watch their cooking: it is impossible to give precise times, as these will depend on the freshness and size of the vegetables. Under-cook them if anything, then take them off the heat and leave them in their cooking water until the moment comes to serve them.

5   To make the sauce, take 250ml *(a scant ½ pint)* of the chicken bouillon and reduce it by two-thirds over a brisk heat. Take it off the heat, add the cream, and bring it back to the boil. Finally, over a brisk heat, whisk in the watercress butter, bit by bit. Pour the sauce into a sauceboat.

Serving

6   You can serve the chicken whole, like a *pot-au-feu*, in a large dish surrounded by the vegetables, or you can cut it into manageable pieces first and then arrange it on a large dish with all the vegetables. Pass the sauce in the sauceboat and serve the bouillon in cups.

Guinea Fowl with Baby Turnips

Pintadeau aux navets nouveaux

For two people

1	young guinea fowl, weighing 400g *(14 oz)*
16	very small new white turnips
80g *(2¾ oz)*	unsalted butter
½	carrot
¼	stick of celery
1	sprig of parsley
	oil
8	cloves of garlic, unpeeled
100ml *(scant ¼ pint)*	vegetable stock (optional; see page 246)
	salt and pepper

Preparation

1   The turnips should still have their green stems attached. Shorten these stems to 6cm *(2⅜ in)* and peel the turnips as if they were apples. Wrap the stems in aluminium foil to protect them and cook the turnips in boiling salted water for 7–10 minutes, according to the quality of the vegetables. Take them out and let them cool.

Unwrap the aluminium foil. Quarter the turnips so that each quarter has a share of green and arrange them in a buttered oven dish. Season them and dot them with 30g *(1 oz)* of the butter, cut into flakes. Set them aside.

2   Make a mirepoix of the carrot and celery, cut into very small cubes.

3   Snip the parsley with scissors; you will need a good teaspoonful.

Cooking and finishing

4   To cook the guinea fowl, pre-heat the oven to 270°C/520°F/ Gas 10. Season the bird, inside and out, with salt and pepper. Brush 10g *(¼ oz)* softened butter over its breast. Heat a teaspoonful of oil in a heavy iron roasting pan that is just big enough to allow the bird to be propped up on its side and, over a moderate heat, lightly colour each side of its breast.

When the two sides are just browned, take the pan off the stove. Leave the bird on its side and arrange the mirepoix around it. Add the unpeeled garlic cloves. Brush another 20g (¾ oz) butter on the top of the bird and roast it in the pre-heated oven.

Give the guinea fowl 10 minutes roasting in all, basting continually and turning the bird on to its other side after 4 minutes. Undo the trussing string after another 4 minutes to free the legs. Roast the bird on its back for the last 2 minutes to finish cooking the legs.

Take the guinea fowl out of the oven, but leave the oven on. Cut the bird in half. Remove all the visible bones (the ribs and back-bones) from the inside. Keep the guinea fowl warm between two soup-plates and set the bones aside. Throw away the fat the bird was cooked in, but keep the mirepoix and garlic in the pan.

5   Slide the buttered turnips, in their dish, into the hot oven. Let them heat through for 5 minutes.

6   To make the sauce, put the roasting pan with the mirepoix and garlic back on to the stove. Break up the guinea fowl bones and put them into the pan. Let them sizzle for a moment, then dilute with 100ml (a scant ¼ pint) water or vegetable stock. Cook for 5 minutes, crushing the bones to extract all the juices. Press the sauce through a sieve into a small saucepan. Season it to taste, reheat it and whisk in the last 20g (¾ oz) butter. Add the parsley.

Serving

7   Arrange two rows of turnip quarters in a half-circle on two heated plates, stems outwards. Place the half guinea fowl in the centre and coat it with the sauce.

Roast Duck with Salsify

Canard rôti aux salsifis

For two people

1	duck, weighing 1.5kg *(3½ lb)*
4	salsifies
1	small shallot
2	cloves of garlic
	flat parsley
2 tbsps	oil
100g *(3½ oz)*	unsalted butter
3 tbsps	red wine vinegar
3 tbsps	white port (see editor's note, page 9)
	salt and pepper

Preparation

1 The duck should have its giblets with it; keep the liver and heart. Shorten the wings by removing the tips. Remove as much fat as you can from the inside. Season the bird inside and out, and truss it.

2 Peel the salsifies. Cut off the ends and slice them into sticks 3cm *(1⅛ in)* long and 5mm *(³⁄₁₆ in)* wide.

3 Peel the shallot and chop it very finely.

4 Peel the cloves of garlic and chop them very finely indeed.

5 Chop the parsley; you will need enough to fill 1 dessertspoon.

6 Cut the duck liver and heart into quite small pieces.

Cooking and finishing

7 To cook the duck, pre-heat the oven to 260°C/500°F/ Gas 10. Heat 1 tablespoon of oil in a very hot roasting pan. Put the duck into the pan on its side. Cook it over a high heat for 2 minutes. Turn it over and cook it on its other side for another 2 minutes. This is to brown it and to start the fat running.

131

Roast the duck immediately in the pre-heated oven, still on its side; it will need 20 minutes altogether. Turn it on to its other side after 8 minutes and let it roast for the last 4 minutes on its back. Take it out of the oven and put in on to a plate for at least 10 minutes before serving.

8 To cook the salsify, while the duck is cooking, fry the little salsify sticks briskly in 1 tablespoon of oil for about 2 minutes, then lower the heat to medium and continue cooking, shaking the pan and turning the salsify from time to time, for 7 minutes more. Add salt, pepper and a nut of butter. Give the salsify 12–15 minutes cooking in all, then set it aside.

9 To make the sauce, melt 20g *(¾ oz)* of the butter in a small saucepan. Add the garlic and shallot and let them sweat for 3 minutes over a medium heat. Add the vinegar and the port and let it 'draw' for 1 minute. Remove the pan from the heat.

Pour all the juice that has collected inside the duck into the sauce. Season the sauce with salt and pepper and thicken it by gradually whisking in 30g *(1 oz)* cold, diced butter, then add no more than a few drops of fresh vinegar. Heat the sauce to bubbling point again, then add the chopped parsley. Set the sauce aside.

10 For garnish, quickly sauté the duck liver and heart in 10g *(¼ oz)* hot butter; 30 seconds is long enough.

Serving

11 Bring the duck to the table whole, surrounded by the salsify. Pour a little sauce over the duck and strew it with little bits of fried liver and heart. Save some liver and heart to add to the sauce; serve the sauce in a sauceboat.

Duck with Spring Vegetables

Caneton printanier

For two people

1	duck, weighing 1.5kg *(3½ lb)*
2	young turnips, each weighing about 100g *(3½ oz)*
6	new-season onions, with green
50g *(2 oz)*	*petits pois*, shelled
50g *(2 oz)*	very young haricot beans, stringed
50g *(2 oz)*	mangetout peas, stringed
1 tbsp	oil
50g *(2 oz)*	sugar
2 tbsps	sherry vinegar
3 tbsps	white stock (see page 244)
150ml *(¼ pint)*	veal stock (see page 247)
40g *(1½ oz)*	unsalted butter
	salt and pepper

Preparation

1 Peel the turnips as you would apples and divide each one into twelve sections.

2 Shorten the new-season onion stems to 5cm *(2 in)*. Remove the outer skins if they are tough.

3 Cut the mangetout peas and the beans into 15mm *(½ in)* pieces.

4 Bring a pan of salted water to the boil, throw in the beans, then, 2–3 minutes later, add the *petits pois*. Add the mangetouts shortly afterwards – they will be cooked in 2 minutes. After making sure that all the vegetables are cooked *al dente*, drain them and set them aside.

5 Blanch the onions for 5 minutes in boiling salted water. Drain them.

6 Clean the duck and shorten the wings by one joint. Season it inside, after removing as much fat from within as you can.

Cooking and finishing

7 To cook the duck, pre-heat the oven to 260°C/500°F/Gas 10. Season the outside of the duck. Make a tablespoon of oil very hot in a roasting pan. Put the duck into it on its side and brown it. Turn it on to its other side after 2 minutes. Cook for another 2 minutes to brown it well and start the fat running.

Put the roasting pan in the pre-heated oven, giving the duck 8 minutes on its left side, 8 on its right and 4 on its back. Take it out and keep it hot on a plate. Give the meat time to rest before serving. Pour the fat out of the roasting pan.

8 For the preliminary cooking of the turnips, while the duck is cooking, season the pieces of turnip, then fry them in a little oil, stirring them until they take a light colour on both sides.

9 For the base of the sauce, put 50g *(1¾ oz)* of the sugar into a saucepan over a fairly low heat. It will melt, then caramelise. Dilute it (with care, as it will spit) with the vinegar, white stock and 3 tablespoons of the veal stock. Cook it for 3–4 minutes.

10 Finish cooking the turnips by plunging them into the half-prepared sauce. Bring it to a good boil and cook the turnips for 3 minutes. Take the pan off the heat and remove the turnips to a plate with a slotted spoon. Set them aside. Add 20g *(¾ oz)* butter to the sauce and let it melt gently. Adjust the seasoning with salt and pepper.

11 While the duck is cooking, finish the other vegetables by heating them gently in a little melted butter. Keep the onions hot in one little pan, and the mixture of peas, beans and mangetouts in another, away from the heat. Do not forget to season both.

12 Glaze the duck by deglazing the roasting pan with the remaining veal stock. Bring it to the boil. Add 20g *(¾ oz)* butter and 6 tablespoons of the caramelised sauce. Mix and stir well, and put the duck into the pan. Make it shiny by basting continually for 2 minutes with the sauce as it cooks. Take out the duck, pouring the juice that has collected inside it into the saucepan containing the sauce. Put the duck on to a long, hot serving dish.

13 Finish the sauce by adding the contents of the roasting pan to the saucepan. Taste and adjust the seasoning for the last time. If the sauce is too thick, thin it with a little dry white wine. Bring it to the boil for the last time and put the turnips into it again.

Serving

14 Pour the sauce all around the duck, arranging the turnip sections all around it too. Put three buttered onions at each end and neatly place the green vegetables here and there. Serve immediately.

Boned Stuffed Pigeons St Francis
Coeur de pigeon Saint-François

For four people

4	pigeons, with giblets (see editor's note, page 7)
1	shallot
160–200g *(6–7 oz)*	veal sweetbreads
50–60g *(1¾–2¼ oz)*	truffles (see editor's note, page 8)
100g *(3½ oz)*	cooked foie gras (see editor's note, page 6)
60g *(2¼ oz)*	unsalted butter
4	egg yolks
4 tbsps	Madeira
	salt and pepper

Preparation

1 Remove the heads, wing tips, feet and guts of the pigeons. Bone them in the following way: lay each bird, breast down, on the table. Cut along the middle of the back as far as the parson's nose. Remove the parson's nose, then, with a small and very sharp knife, carefully detach the meat from the bones. First work down one side of the ribs and then work along the other side. Cut through the hip and shoulder joints. Finally, take the meat from either side of the breast-bone, but leave the cartilage in place for the time being so that the legs, wings, skin and breast meat remain in one piece and the carcass can be taken right out. Remove the gizzard, liver and heart from the carcass.

2 Now bone the wings and thighs. Work on each limb in turn, by arranging the boned birds so that you can gently push the meat from the ends of the severed joints. When the bones are bared you can cut them off at the next joints. Collect any meat that still clings to the bones after you have detached them and set it aside. Collect the meat from the thighs.

3 The pigeons are now completely boned and flat on the table. All that remains to be done is carefully to remove the cartilaginous pieces of breast-bone and lumps of fat around the rumps. The boned birds are now ready for stuffing. (Keep the bones to help make the gravy.)

4 To prepare the stuffing, open the gizzards and empty them. Keep only the meaty parts: peel away the skins. Chop the meat into small pieces. Chop the hearts, livers and reserved thigh meat. Peel and chop the shallot. Cut the raw sweetbreads into dice 1cm *(⅜ in)* square. Season them with salt and pepper. Cut the truffles into little dice.

5 Heat a large nut of butter in a frying pan and quickly sauté the diced, seasoned sweetbreads, turning them constantly with a spatula. After 1½ minutes, add the liver, heart, gizzard and chopped pigeon meat. Season and add the shallot. Stir for 1 minute more, then add the diced truffle and 20g *(¾ oz)* butter. Let it cook for another minute, then take the pan off the heat and taste for seasoning.

6 Take half the mixture that you have just prepared, put it into a food processor with half the foie gras and make it into a soft purée. Cut the rest of the foie gras into dice.

7 Mix the puréed stuffing with the stuffing that has been left unprocessed. Add the egg yolks and the diced foie gras. Taste the seasoning and adjust if necessary. The stuffing is now prepared.

To stuff the pigeons, arrange one-quarter of the stuffing in a little dome on the breast of each bird. Fold each of the boned thighs over the stuffing to form a triangular heart shape and sew it up firmly across the top and down the centre.

Cooking and finishing

8 Break up the pigeon bones. You can make a little gravy with them in a saucepan or simply cook them with the birds in the oven to help flavour the juices.

9 Pre-heat the oven to 230°C/450°F/Gas 8. Season the pigeons with salt and pepper and arrange them in a lightly oiled baking dish or a *sautoir*. Heat gently on top of the stove so that each side of the pigeon 'hearts' is lightly browned.

10 The cooking proper is then continued in the pre-heated oven. Roast the pigeons for 15 minutes, basting them often and turning them over half-way through their cooking time.

11 Remove the pigeons when they are done and arrange them on a serving dish. Deglaze the baking dish with the Madeira and 4 tablespoons of water, or, if the truffles were tinned, with 4 tablespoons of truffle juice. Scrape the pan for the juices and sediment (first removing the pigeon bones, if you used them). Let the gravy bubble up once or twice, then strain it into a sauceboat.

Serving

12 Serve the pigeon 'hearts' (having first removed the threads) on a serving dish or on heated plates, with the gravy in its sauceboat.

Pot-au-feu of Pigeon

Pot-au-feu de pigeon

Editor's note – The Pinot sauce is optional, as it is intended to go with the foie gras – although the sauce is still very good with the pigeon even if you decide to forgo the foie gras.

For two people

1	pigeon, weighing 400g *(14 oz)* or 2 pigeons weighing 240g *(8 oz)* (see editor's note, page 7)
125g *(4½ oz)*	raw duck foie gras (optional; see editor's note, page 6)
4	medium-sized carrots
4	young turnips
2	new-season onions, with stems
1	small savoy cabbage
4	cloves of garlic
10g *(¼ oz)*	unsalted butter
1 litre *(1¾ pints)*	white stock (see page 244)
4	slices of French bread
	oil
	salt and pepper

Pinot sauce (optional)

1	shallot
70g *(2½ oz)*	unsalted butter
200ml *(scant ½ pint)*	Pinot Noir *or* good red wine
3 tbsps	brown stock (see page 244)
	sugar
	red wine vinegar
	salt and pepper

Preparation

1   Shape the carrots and turnips into neat spindles 4–5cm *(1½–2 in)* long.

2   Peel the onions and shorten the stems to 3cm *(1⅛ in)*. Slice the discarded green stems very finely; you will need 2 tablespoonsful of sliced stems.

3   Throw away the coarsest outer leaves of the cabbage. Cut the core out of the cabbage with a sharp vegetable knife, leaving a cone-shaped hole in the centre. Remove the leaves one by one. Cut the central rib out of the largest leaves (keep the smallest ones for a different recipe).

4 Peel the cloves of garlic.

5 To prepare the Pinot sauce (see editor's note above), peel and finely chop the shallot. Put it, with 20g *(¾ oz)* of the butter, into a small saucepan over a medium heat. When the butter froths, add the wine and the brown stock. Reduce until the liquid thickens enough to just coat the back of a spoon. Set this reduction aside.

Cooking and finishing

6 To cook the pot-au-feu, season the white stock and bring it just to the boil. Put the pigeon in it and poach it, just simmering but not boiling at all, for 25 minutes. 5 minutes before the end, add the foie gras in one slice.

7 Meanwhile, cook the carrots, turnips and onions in a little boiling salted water to which you have added a nut of butter. Take care not to over-cook the vegetables – they must remain firm. Keep them warm in their cooking liquid.

8 Cook the cabbage leaves in boiling salted water for about 10 minutes. Drain them, but do not refresh them; wrap them at once in a cloth and squeeze it well to press out all the water, pressing the leaves together in a tight ball.

9 Fry the cloves of garlic in a pan with a drop of oil, adding 10g *(¼ oz)* butter and seasoning them with salt as they turn golden. Set them aside and keep them warm.

10 Toast the slices of bread.

11 To finish the sauce, reheat the reduction of wine and whisk in 50g *(1¾ oz)* butter. Season with salt, pepper, a pinch of sugar and a few drops of vinegar. Put the sauce in a sauceboat.

Serving

12 Put the whole pigeon and the whole piece of foie gras into a soup tureen with the cabbage ball and the little vegetables. Pour some of the pigeon's cooking bouillon over them. Sprinkle the sliced onion stems on top.

Serve the sauce in a sauceboat. The toasted bread, each slice surmounted by a clove of garlic, should be on a little plate.

At the table, cut the pigeon in half. Put one portion on each plate, with half the foie gras (cut slantwise) and half the vegetables. Cut the cabbage ball in half. Coat the portions of foie gras with the Pinot sauce. Serve the bouillon separately in little bowls. Put the little plate of garlic toast on the table.

Pigeon with Cabbage

Pigeon au chou

For two people

1	pigeon, weighing 400g *(14 oz)* or 2 pigeons weighing 240g *(8 oz)* (see editor's note, page 7)
6	large leaves from a Savoy cabbage
2	thin rashers of bacon
1	new-season onion
3	cloves of garlic
60g *(2¼ oz)*	unsalted butter
1 tsp	oil
5 tbsps	white stock (see page 244)
	chopped parsley
	salt and pepper

Preparation

1 Remove the central rib from the cabbage leaves. Blanch the leaves for 1 minute in boiling salted water. Refresh them in cold water and drain them.

2 Cut the bacon into very thin strips.

3 Chop the onion finely.

4 Peel the cloves of garlic, but leave them whole.

Cooking and finishing

5 To cook the pigeon, pre-heat the oven to 270°C/520°F/ Gas 10. Season the pigeon with salt and pepper. Brush 10g *(½ oz)* softened butter over the breast and colour each side lightly by cooking it first on one side and then on the other in a little frying pan or heavy iron gratin dish. To avoid burning the butter, add a teaspoon of oil and use a moderate heat.

6   As soon as the breast is a light golden colour, remove the pan from the heat. Keep the pigeon on its side, add the garlic and brush 20g *(1 oz)* butter on the uppermost side of the bird, to keep it moist. Put it into the pre-heated oven.

7   Baste the bird often, turning it over after 3 minutes. Roast it for another 3 minutes with the other side uppermost, then give it 1 minute on its back. If the bird was trussed, cut the trussing string to release the thighs.

8   When the bird has roasted for 7 minutes in all, take it out of the pan or gratin dish. Throw away the fat but keep the cloves of garlic.

9   Cut up the pigeon. Take the legs and the breasts off the carcass. Leave the wings attached to the breast fillets. Keep these pieces of pigeon warm between two soup-plates.

10 To cook the cabbage, cut each blanched and drained cabbage leaf into three or four pieces. Melt a large nut of butter in a frying pan over a gentle heat and add the strips of bacon and the chopped onion. As soon as the butter foams, add the cabbage. Season with salt and pepper and leave it to cook for 6–8 minutes, still over a low heat.

11 To make the sauce, break the carcass into several pieces and put them back into the roasting pan or dish along with the cloves of garlic. Add the white stock and 3 tablespoons of water. Cook over a brisk heat for 5 minutes, crushing the bones to obtain as much flavour as possible.

12 Take the bones out of the pan. Push the liquid through a fine sieve. Leave the sieved juices in a small saucepan.

13 To finish the sauce, put the small saucepan with its sieved juices back on to the stove. Bring it to the boil, then whisk in 10g *(¼ oz)* butter and taste for seasoning. If necessary, dilute the sauce with a spoonful of water. Add a pinch of chopped parsley and remove the sauce from the heat.

Serving

14 Divide the cabbage between two heated plates. Heap it in the centre of each plate and arrange the pigeon pieces on top, coated with the sauce.

Rabbit with Mustard

Emincé de lapin à la moutarde

This recipe uses the back legs of a rabbit in a way that makes a change from the more usual rabbit *en gibelotte*, or stew.

For three or four people

	the forepart and back legs taken from a rabbit weighing 2.5kg *(5½ lb)*
1	small shallot
40g *(1½ oz)*	unsalted butter
1 tbsp	Dijon mustard
3 tbsps	dry white wine
1 tsp	veal stock (see page 247)
3 tbsps	double cream
1 tsp	mustard powder
	salt and pepper

Preparation

1 Pull the tendons from the rabbit legs. Bone the meat and cut it into pieces measuring 2 × 1cm *(¾ × ⅜ in)*.

2 Peel and chop the shallot.

Finishing and serving

3 Season the rabbit pieces with salt and pepper.

4 Heat the butter in a frying pan over a moderate heat. Add the rabbit and the shallot and stir for about 2 minutes while the meat firms up, then put the meat on to a plate and keep it warm.

5 Add the mustard to the frying pan and let it sizzle, stirring with a spatula. Next, deglaze the pan with the white wine and add the stock. Mix well and let it reduce by two-thirds, or until the sauce thickens enough to lightly coat the back of a spoon. Add the cream and continue reducing, briskly, until the sauce is reduced by a good half. Set it aside.

6 Add to the sauce the juices that have in the meantime run from the rabbit. Stir the teaspoonful of mustard powder into the sauce. Mix well. Finally, put the pieces of rabbit into the sauce and heat them through, but do not let them cook any more. Taste for seasoning and serve.

Saddle of Rabbit with Basil

Râble de lapin au basilic

This was the main dish at the luncheon to celebrate my Gault-Millau *Clé d'Or* award in 1975.

The recipe uses only the saddle of the rabbit; use the rest of it to make either the Rabbit with Mustard (see page 142) or the Feuilletés of Rabbit and Basil (see page 59). The liver can be used for Feuilletés of Rabbit Liver and Leeks (see page 58) or Rabbit Titbits with Morels and Truffles (see page 56).

For three people

1	saddle from a rabbit weighing 2.5kg *(5½ lb)*; the saddle should weigh about 450g *(1 lb)*
1	bunch of basil
4	shallots
1 tbsp	oil
6	cloves of garlic, unpeeled
100ml *(scant ¼ pint)*	white wine *or* chicken stock (see page 243)
1 tbsp	veal stock (see page 247) *or* meat gravy
50g *(1¾ oz)*	unsalted butter
	salt and pepper

Preparation

1 Snip the basil with scissors. You will need 2 heaped tablespoonsful.

2 Peel the shallots and cut them into quarters.

3 Trim the saddle, then make two deep cuts, down to the bone, along either side of the back-bone. Stuff half the basil into these cuts. Season the meat with salt and pepper.

Cooking and finishing

4 To cook the sadddle, pre-heat the oven to 180°C/350°F/ Gas 4. Heat a tablespoon of oil in a roasting pan; do not let it get too hot. Arrange the saddle in it, with the unpeeled cloves of garlic and the shallots. Turn the rabbit over on all sides – this is not to cook it, but simply to blanch the meat; it should just lose its redness.

5   Put the pan and its contents into the pre-heated oven. Baste and turn the meat frequently, taking care that the saddle does not brown. Cook it for 12 minutes, then take it out of the pan. If your oven is a well-insulated commercial one, turn it off; if not, reduce the temperature to 130°C/270°F/ Gas ½. Put the saddle into another oven dish and return it to the oven while you make the sauce.

6   To make the sauce, put the original oven dish, with its garlic, shallots and cooking juices, on to a high heat and let the contents colour a little. Deglaze with the wine or chicken stock and the veal stock or meat gravy. Cook it for a few minutes more, until the garlic and shallot are soft.

7   Push everything through a small sieve into a small saucepan. Reduce the sieved juices a little on a low heat. Add the rest of the basil and thicken the sauce by gradually whisking in 50g *(1¾ oz)* cold, diced butter. Taste for seasoning.

Serving

8   Carve the saddle along its length. Serve it with a purée of vegetables and a *Paillasson* of Potatoes (see page 189).

Meat and Offal

Veal with a Fricassée of Artichokes and Petits Pois

Emincé de veau à la fricassée d'artichauts et petits pois

This recipe is none other than the well-known Swiss speciality *l'émincé de veau à la Zürichoise.* Contrary to what is often thought, it contains no cream.

For two people

250g *(9 oz)*	veal, taken from the *noix* (rump or topside) or the fillet
4	cooked artichoke hearts (see page 177) with their cooking liquid
4 tbsps	*petits pois,* cooked
	parsley
1	shallot
1	new-season onion
	oil
90g *(3 oz)*	butter
100ml *(scant ¼ pint)*	white wine
	salt and pepper

Preparation

1 Cut the meat into slices about 5mm *(³⁄₁₆ in)* thick and then into pieces 1 × 2cm *(³⁄₈ × ¾ in).*

2 If need be, trim the artichoke hearts and cut them into quarters. Reserve 2 tablespoons of their cooking liquid. If you have no *petits pois* already cooked, cook them now.

147

3 Snip the parsley with scissors; you will need a good teaspoonful. Peel and chop the shallot finely; you will need 1 tablespoonful. Slice the onion; you will need 1 tablespoonful.

Finishing

4 Lightly oil a frying pan and make it very hot. Season the meat with salt and pepper and sauté briskly, while stirring, for 30 seconds. Add the chopped shallot and 30g *(1 oz)* butter. Continue cooking and stirring for another 30 seconds, then remove the meat with a slotted spoon. Set it aside.

5 Deglaze the pan with the white wine. Scrape the bottom well to collect all the juices. Reduce them over a brisk heat for 2 minutes. Add the sliced onion and gradually whisk 30g *(1 oz)* cold, diced butter into the sauce. Return the pieces of veal to the pan. Keep it warm at the side of the stove, but do not let it cook any more. Taste for seasoning.

6 To cook the fricassée of vegetables, reheat the quartered artichoke hearts in 2 tablespoons of their cooking liquid. Add 30g *(1 oz)* butter and the cooked *petits pois*. Let the artichokes colour slightly.

Serving

7 Arrange the artichoke quarters and the *petits pois* like a little crown around the veal on heated plates. Sprinkle the parsley over the veal.

Veal 'au Curry'

Emincé de veau au curry

I like curry very much. Unfortunately, it is too often used to camouflage food that is past its best.

For four people

500g *(1 lb 2 oz)*	veal from the *noix* (the rump or topside) or the fillet
4 heaped tsps	good curry powder
	oil
30g *(1 oz)*	unsalted butter
150ml *(¼ pint)*	dry white wine
300ml *(½ pint)*	double cream
	lemon juice
	salt and pepper
	roasted almonds } to garnish the veal (optional)
	fried onion rings }
	diced red *or* green peppers } to decorate the
	petits pois, cooked } accompanying rice
	raisins, soaked } pilaff (optional)

Preparation

1 Cut the veal into slices about 5mm *(¼ in)* thick, then cut it into pieces measuring 1 × 2cm *(⅜ × ¾ in)*. Put the meat into a bowl.

2 Prepare the garnishes if you are having them.

Finishing

3 Sprinkle the meat with the curry powder (use less if you like your curry mild). Add salt and pepper and mix well with your hands to make sure that all the pieces of meat are well seasoned.

4 Using a non-stick pan, make a little splash of oil very, very hot. Add the veal and, without delay, separate the pieces as they cook, using a wooden fork. After 30 seconds, add 30g *(1 oz)* butter, and let the meat colour lightly for 1 minute. The meat should cover the pan in one layer.

5 Take the meat out of the pan with a slotted spoon and put it aside on a plate.

6 Deglaze the pan with the white wine and reduce it by two-thirds over a brisk heat. Add the cream and continue the reduction, boiling fast until the sauce thickens enough to coat the back of a spoon. Set it aside.

7 Put the meat back into the sauce for long enough to reheat it, but do not let it cook any more. Taste for seasoning, add a dash of lemon juice and serve immediately.

Serving

8 Garnish the veal with roasted almonds and fried onion rings. Accompany this curry with a rice pilaff, embellished, if you like, with little dice of raw sweet pepper, soaked raisins and cooked peas.

Noisettes of Veal à la Hongroise

Noisettes de veau à la hongroise

For four people

600g *(1 lb 5 oz)*	veal, taken from the *filet mignon* or *carré* (the best end of neck or the centre of the fillet), cut into 12 small slices
1	red pepper
	oil
60g *(2¼ oz)*	unsalted butter
4 tsps	good-quality paprika
½ tsp	dried chilli pepper, crushed
300ml *(½ pint)*	double cream
	lemon juice
	slivered almonds
	parsley, snipped
	salt and pepper

Preparation

1 If this has not already been done by the butcher, cut the veal into twelve small, equal-sized slices or *noisettes*.

2 Remove the seeds and cut the white parts from the red pepper. Cut it into strips 2mm *(1/16 in)* wide, then cut these strips into tiny cubes. You will need 4 tablespoonsful.

Finishing

3 Season the *noisettes* with salt and pepper. Heat 1 tablespoon of oil in a frying pan. When the oil is very hot, put the *noisettes* into the pan and cook them briskly for exactly 1 minute, turning them as they cook. Then reduce the heat. Add 50g *(1¾ oz)* butter. Add the paprika. Let the butter froth up. Take the *noisettes* out of the pan with a slotted spoon and set them aside to keep warm.

4 To make the sauce, add no more crushed chilli pepper than can be picked up on the point of a knife, per person, as this dish is very spicy. Mix it with the buttery juices in the pan, then deglaze with 3 tablespoons of water. Let the liquid bubble up once or twice over a good heat to reduce it a little, then add the cream. Scrape the bottom of the pan very well and let the sauce reduce until it is thick enough to coat the back of a spoon. Taste for seasoning.

5 Return the *noisettes* to the sauce, with any juice that may have run from them. Let the sauce bubble up once more, then set the pan aside, adding a dash of lemon juice at the last moment to enliven the sauce.

6 To cook the red pepper, heat a drop of oil in a frying pan and briskly sauté the little dice. Drain off the oil.

Serving

7 Line up three *noisettes* in the middle of each heated plate. Scatter a little of the diced red pepper over them, then coat both pepper and *noisettes* with the sauce. Garnish with a few slivered almonds and some snipped parsley.

Sautéed Fillet of Veal with Swiss Chard

Pièce de veau poêlée aux bettes

For two people

1	slice of veal fillet, weighing 300g *(10½ oz)*
2	medium-sized shallots
4	large Swiss chard leaves
150ml *(¼ pint)*	red Bordeaux wine
200ml *(scant ½ pint)*	veal stock (see page 247)
	oil
	olive oil
1	sprig of thyme
60g *(2¼ oz)*	butter
3 tbsps	double cream
	salt and pepper

Preparation

1 Peel the shallots and chop them finely.

2 Wash the Swiss chard leaves. Cut off the green parts and cut them into three or four pieces, having removed the largest veins. Pull all the strings and outer membranes from the main central ribs. Cut the ribs into thin slices, 5mm *(³⁄₁₆ in)* wide. Blanch the leaves in boiling salted water for 3 minutes. Drain them and dry them on a cloth.

3 Prepare a reduction of the red wine by simmering it with half the shallots in a small saucepan. When it has the consistency of a thick syrup, add the veal stock. Reduce it again by a good third, over a brisk fire.

Cooking and finishing

4 Season the meat with salt and pepper and sauté it gently in oil for 7 minutes, turning it over several times. Drain off the oil and replace it with 20g *(¾ oz)* of the butter. Add 1 level tablespoon of chopped shallot and continue cooking over a gentle heat for about 3 minutes, frequently basting the meat with the melted butter.

5   At the same time, begin to cook the sliced chard ribs. Put them into a frying pan with a few drops of olive oil and a pinch of thyme. Do not cook them for more than 6 minutes, as the pieces must remain firm. Season with salt and pepper at the end of the cooking time and at the same time add 20g *(¾ oz)* butter.

6   Roughly chop the blanched and dried chard leaves. Put them into a saucepan with 20g *(¾ oz)* butter. Let them just soften over a medium heat. Season them with salt and pepper and add the cream. Let them cook for a few moments more, gently simmering, until the cream thickens of its own accord.

7   Reheat the red wine reduction and add it to the butter in which the veal has cooked.

Serving

8   Arrange the fricassée of chard ribs on a round dish with the leaves heaped in the centre. Cut the piece of veal on the slant in slices 1cm *(⅜ in)* thick, as if it were an entrecôte. Reassemble the fillet and arrange it on the bed of chard leaves. Coat it lightly with some of the sauce. Serve the rest of the sauce in a sauceboat.

Mignonnette of Lamb with Parsley and Mushroom

Mignonnette d'agneau au persil et champignons

You will find that parsley used as a vegetable (as it is in this recipe) is excellent.

For four people

4	thick *mignonnettes*, taken from a filleted saddle of lamb, each weighing 180g *(6½ oz)*
400g *(14 oz)*	curled parsley, without stalks
1	clove of garlic
1	shallot
400g *(14 oz)*	small cultivated mushrooms
80g *(2¾ oz)*	unsalted butter
200ml *(scant ½ pint)*	double cream
	oil
	salt and pepper

Preparation

1 Blanch the parsley in boiling salted water for 6 minutes. Drain it and dry it thoroughly in a cloth.

2 Peel and chop the garlic and the shallot finely. Keep them separate.

3 Clean the mushrooms and, if they are large, halve or quarter them.

Finishing

4 To cook the parsley, put 50g *(1¾ oz)* of the butter into a frying pan with the shallot. Heat it and when the butter foams add the parsley. Separate it with a fork. Add the cream and let it bubble up twice, so that it is absorbed by the parsley. Season with salt and pepper and remove from the heat.

5 To cook the mushrooms, put 1 tablespoon of oil into a non-stick pan. Add the mushrooms and let them colour lightly over a brisk heat. When they have given out their juice, add 30g *(1 oz)* butter, the chopped garlic, salt and pepper. Mix well and continue cooking until the mushrooms are well coloured. Remove the pan from the heat.

6 To cook the *mignonnettes*, season them and fry them in oil
for 7–8 minutes. Use a medium heat from the beginning.

Serving

7 Carve the *mignonnettes* into slices and arrange them on
heated plates in a circle around the parsley, which is
heaped in the middle. Scatter the mushrooms over the
meat.

Noisettes of Lamb with Truffle and Lyonnaise Potatoes

Noisettes d'agneau à la truffe et pommes Lyonnaise

Editor's note – This recipe, which takes no time at all to cook, can be
adapted for more than one person by an appropriate increase of all
the ingredients except the egg yolk, which will glaze enough
noisettes for six. Take care, too, to use frying pans that are large
enough to allow plenty of room for tossing and turning the *noisettes*
and the Lyonnaise potatoes.

You could substitute mushroom for truffle but, as Fredy Girardet
would say, it won't be the same.

For one person

2–3	*noisettes*, each 3cm *(1⅜ in)* thick, taken from a filleted saddle of lamb
2–3	sprigs of parsley
20g *(¾ oz)*	truffle (see editor's note, page 8)
100g *(3½ oz)*	new potatoes
20g *(¾ oz)*	finely sliced onion rings
1	egg yolk
	oil
15g *(½ oz)*	unsalted butter
1 tbsp	veal glaze (see page 247)
	salt and pepper

Preparation

1 Chop the parsley very finely; you will need
2 tablespoonsful.

2 Chop the truffle finely. Set a quarter of it aside for the sauce
and mix the rest with the parsley.

3 Using a mandoline, slice the potatoes 2mm *(¹⁄₁₆ in)* thick. Separate the onion slices into rings.

4 Put the egg yolk into a little bowl. It is to be used as if for pastry glaze, so mix it with 1 teaspoon of water.

Finishing

5 Season the *noisettes*. Brush each one with the egg yolk, then roll them in the parsley-and-truffle mixture, pressing well to make it stick.

6 Heat a little oil in a non-stick frying pan. Add the *noisettes*. Let them cook for 3 minutes, turning them once or twice. Add the butter and take the pan off the heat for 2 minutes to let it 'draw', then put the *noisettes* on to a heated plate. Set the pan and its juices aside.

7 Cook the Lyonnaise potatoes at the same time as you cook the meat. Cook them in a large frying pan, in very hot oil, for 5 minutes in all, turning them often. Add the onion rings half-way through cooking.

8 To make the sauce, add the rest of the truffle and a scant tablespoonful of the veal glaze to the juices in the pan in which you cooked the meat. Let the mixture bubble up once. Season with salt and pepper.

Serving

9 Arrange the potatoes in the centre of a heated plate. Put the *noisettes* on top and pour the sauce all round.

Saddle of Lamb with Mustard Seed

Selle d'agneau à la graine de moutarde

This recipe provides the rather agreeable sensation of mustard seeds bursting in your mouth.

For two people

1	small saddle of lamb, weighing 800g *(1¾ lb)* after being severely trimmed of the lower parts of its cutlet bones and all superfluous fat
1	shallot
	fresh green herbs (parsley, chives, chervil, etc.)
1 tbsp	oil
4	cloves of garlic, unpeeled
1	sprig of thyme
1	sprig of rosemary
100g *(3½ oz)*	unsalted butter
2 tbsps	strong mustard
1 tbsp	mustard seeds
	salt and pepper

Preparation

1 Peel and finely chop the shallot. Snip the fresh green herbs with scissors; you will need about 2 tablespoonsful. Use whichever herbs you like, or are in season.

Cooking and finishing

2 To cook the meat, pre-heat the oven to 250°C/480°F/Gas 9. Season the saddle of lamb with salt and pepper. Heat 1 tablespoon of oil in a roasting pan over a high heat. Add the saddle, the unpeeled garlic, thyme and rosemary, and sear the meat rapidly, turning it on all sides in the hot oil. Next, place a nut of butter on the meat with the saddle the right way up and put the roasting pan into the pre-heated oven.

Turn the oven down to 225°C/450°F/Gas 8 after about 10 minutes. Baste the meat frequently, adding another nut of butter twice during its roasting time, which should take about 20 minutes.

3   Take the meat out of the oven and transfer it to a dish that you can keep hot. Add 50–60g *(1¾–2¼ oz)* of the butter to the meat and leave it to rest for about 10 minutes, basting it often with the melting butter.

4   To make the gravy, deglaze the roasting pan with 2 tablespoons of water, scraping the pan well to loosen the sediment. Crush the cloves of garlic and press the contents of the pan through a sieve into a small saucepan. Keep it warm.

5   To make the mustard sauce: when the saddle has had its 10 minutes' rest, collect all the buttery juices from the dish and put them in a small frying pan with the chopped shallot and the 2 tablespoons of mustard. Put the pan over a brisk heat and whisk without stopping until the mustard appears to curdle and become granular. Add 10g *(¼ oz)* butter. Let it foam, then add the mustard seeds. Let it just simmer, then add the snipped green herbs. Pour the sauce on to the saddle, spreading it all over the surface as you do so.

Serving

6   Serve the saddle on a serving dish coated with the mustard sauce. Pass the gravy in a sauceboat.

Veal Sweetbreads with Port and Caper Sauce
Noix de ris de veau au porto et aux câpres

The capers give a touch of sharpness, like vinegar.

For two people

2	lobes of veal sweetbread, each weighing about 250g *(9 oz)*
	oil
50g *(1¾ oz)*	unsalted butter
6 tsps	capers
100ml *(scant ¼ pint)*	white port (see editor's note, page 9)
3 tbsps	veal stock (see page 247)
	lemon juice
	salt and pepper

Preparation

1 Soak the sweetbreads under a trickle of running water for 3–4 hours.

2 After soaking, skin the sweetbreads delicately and carefully with a kitchen knife, removing all the coarsest membranes, threads and tough bits, but leaving the finest inner skin intact. Cut the sweetbreads in half horizontally, so that you now have four slices.

Finishing

3 Season the sweetbreads with salt and pepper. Using a non-stick pan, make a drop of oil very hot. Briskly 'seize' the sweetbreads in it, giving each side 3 minutes. Remove the pan from the heat. Drain off the oil.

4 Add the butter to the pan and return it to the heat. As soon as it froths, take the pan off the heat. Keep it at one side of the stove and, without cooking the butter, baste the sweetbreads with it for 2 minutes.

5 Finally, incorporate the capers, port and veal stock. Put the pan back on to the stove, add a little squeeze of lemon juice and very quickly make it bubble up just once.

6 Away from the stove, baste the sweetbreads again several times with the sauce. Taste for seasoning and adjust it if necessary.

Serving

7 Serve the sweetbreads on heated plates, coated with the sauce.

Veal Kidney Bolo

Rognon de veau Bolo

This dish used to be made by my father in a restaurant in Lausanne for his old friend Bolo Pacha. Bolo wanted his kidney cooked only in butter, in an iron egg-dish.

The whole secret of success lies on the one hand in the quality of the kidney and on the other in speedy cooking. For this reason it is best to cook the kidneys a few at a time. For four people, for example, you should make two servings, cooking the second batch when the first has been eaten.

Editor's note – It is not always easy to find veal kidneys with their bed of fat still round them. Give your butcher good notice that this is how you want them, as the fat is important for its flavour.

For two people

1	large veal kidney, encased in good white fat
2 tsps	olive oil
40g *(1¼ oz)*	unsalted butter
	salt and pepper

Preparation

1　Trim the fat from the kidney, leaving a little coat of fat 5mm *(³⁄₁₆ in)* thick all round, so that it looks like a large white sausage. Cut the kidney into slices 5mm *(³⁄₁₆ in)* thick.

Finishing

2　Make the olive oil very hot in an enamelled, cast-iron egg-dish (the flat kind with two ears), which should be big enough to allow the slices of kidney to lie in one layer without overlapping.

3　When the oil is smoking, quickly put the kidneys into the dish. Season with salt and pepper. Add the butter, turn the kidneys once and take the pan off the heat. The whole operation should take exactly 1 minute.

Serving

4　Serve immediately on heated plates with the butter foaming.

Sautéed Veal Kidney with Red Wine Sauce
Rognon de veau sauté à la Dôle

You can serve this dish either with the kidneys sliced in half, as given in the recipe below, or the two halves can be cut into 5mm *(³⁄₁₆ in)* slices and re-formed to look like half kidneys when they are served.

For two people

1	large veal kidney, encased in good white fat (see page 160)
1½	shallots
150ml *(¼ pint)*	red wine, preferably Dôle du Valais or Pinot noir
½	clove of garlic
1	sprig of parsley
2	sprigs of fresh thyme
20g *(¾ oz)*	fresh breadcrumbs
1 tbsp	olive oil
200ml *(scant ½ pint)*	veal stock (see page 247)
30g *(1 oz)*	unsalted butter
	sugar
	cognac *or* brandy
	salt and pepper

Preparation

1 Cut the fat from the kidney, leaving only a very thin coat of fat, about 5mm *(³⁄₁₆ in)* thick, all round. Cut the kidney in half lengthways. From each half remove whatever you can of the interior threads, ligaments, tubes, etc.

   Arrange some of the fat taken from the outside of the kidney on an oven dish. Put the two halves of kidney side by side on top of the fat and set them aside.

2 Peel and chop the whole shallot. Put it into a little saucepan with the wine and let it reduce to the consistency of a thick syrup. Set it aside.

3 Finely chop the half clove of garlic and the half shallot. Chop the parsley so that you have 1 teaspoonful. Strip the thyme leaves and chop them. Cook all these aromatics in a small saucepan with 1 tablespoon of hot olive oil for 2 minutes, stirring all the time. Lastly, add the breadcrumbs and set the pan aside.

Finishing

4 Pre-heat the oven to 220°C/425°F/Gas 7. Season the halved kidneys with salt and pepper and put them into the pre-heated oven on their bed of fat. Let the fat melt, without opening the oven door for the first 5 minutes, then baste the kidneys with the melted fat several times. Turn them over after 7 minutes and take them out of the oven after 11 minutes' cooking in all. The blood should be just starting to ooze out. Leave the kidneys on a warm plate to give out some of their juice, then add this juice to the previously prepared reduction of red wine.

5 Put the kidneys on to a shallow heat-proof dish and cover them with the *provençale* (the previously cooked mixture of garlic, shallots, breadcrumbs, etc.). Pre-heat the grill.

6 Put the reduction of red wine and shallot back on to the heat. Add the veal stock. Let it reduce by one-third over a brisk heat, then whisk in 30g *(1 oz)* butter. Adjust the seasoning with salt, pepper, a pinch of sugar and a dash of cognac.

7 Pass the dish of kidneys for a moment under the pre-heated grill, leaving it for just long enough to give the *provençale* a little colour.

Serving

8 Coat the bottoms of two large, heated plates with the sauce and serve one half kidney on each plate.

Game

Breast of Hen Pheasant with Black Radishes

Aile de poule faisane aux radis noirs

As the legs of pheasants are often badly damaged, I use the breasts alone like this.

Editor's note – If black radishes are unobtainable, you could substitute large round red radishes or long white 'moolis' or even ordinary small turnips. All are in season at the same time as pheasant.

For two people

1	hen pheasant, weighing about 900g *(2 lb)*
500g *(1 lb 2 oz)*	black radish
80g *(2¾ oz)*	unsalted butter
3 tbsps	game stock (see page 248)
3 tbsps	dry white wine
3 tbsps	white port (see editor's note, page 9)
	lemon
	salt and freshly crushed black pepper *(mignonnette)* (see editor's note, page 7)

Preparation

1 Shape the radishes to resemble large cloves of garlic, peeling them as you turn them. You should have twelve 'cloves' per person.

2 To cook the radishes, melt half the butter in a saucepan. Cook the radish pieces in it, gently, for 5 minutes, so that they colour slightly. Pour off the butter. Add the game stock, port and white wine to the pan. Season and cook the radishes for another 10 minutes or more, when they should

be tender and the liquid should be syrupy. (If the liquid becomes too thick and begins to stick to the bottom of the pan, add a little water, but the liquid must remain syrupy so that the radishes are, as it were, almost candied. At the end of cooking there should not be more than 6–8 tablespoons of the juice left.) Taste for seasoning, adding salt, pepper and a little lemon juice, then set the pan aside.

3   To remove the pheasant breasts, cut the breast fillets away from the breast-bone and wish-bone, but retain the shoulder joint and the upper wing-bone. Trim all the meat off the wing-bone and cut the end off, so that the exposed bone looks like a little handle.

Cooking and finishing

4   To cook the pheasant, pre-heat the oven to 250°C/480°F/ Gas 9. Season the breast fillets and melt the rest of the butter in an iron gratin dish or heavy frying pan. When it is just beginning to brown, put the breasts into the pan and, basting them frequently, roast them at the front of the oven for 8–10 minutes.

When the breasts are cooked, but still pink and juicy, put them on to a carving board and cut the meat into five or six slices in such a way as to make the breast look like an outspread wing, or fan, with all the slices spreading outwards from the wing-bone, to which they must remain attached.

5   Reheat the radishes.

Serving

6   Arrange each breast in the centre of a heated plate, with the slices fanned out and the radishes forming a semi-circle around them. Coat the radishes with their sauce and sprinkle them generously with the crushed pepper.

Casseroled Partridge with Glazed Carrots and a Coulis of Leeks

Perdreau en casserole aux carottes glacées et coulis de poireaux

For four people

2	partridges, cleaned, trussed and barded, with all their giblets
400g *(14 oz)*	carrots
1	medium-sized onion
400g *(14 oz)*	leeks
3 tbsps	mirepoix (see page 251)
150g *(5½ oz)*	unsalted butter
1	sprig of thyme
100ml *(scant ¼ pint)*	double cream
3 tbsps	good champagne *or* dry white wine
200ml *(scant ½ pint)*	game stock (see page 248)
	salt and pepper

Preparation

1 Peel the carrots. Cut them into rounds, on the slant.

2 Peel and chop the onion.

3 Keep only the white and pale green parts of the leeks. Make two cross-cuts down their entire length towards the root end, then cut them into slices 1cm *(⅜ in)* wide. Separate them to obtain little square pieces.

4 Prepare the mirepoix.

Cooking and finishing

5 Soften the onion in 25g *(1 oz)* of the butter, then add the carrots. Season and let them colour lightly. Add water to come half-way up their height. Cover and cook them very gently for 20 minutes. Set them aside and keep them warm.

6 Season the sliced leeks and sauté them briskly in 25g *(1 oz)* butter for 2 minutes. Add 100ml *(a scant ¼ pint)* water. Let it evaporate completely, add the cream and continue to cook for 1 minute, when the cream should coat the leeks nicely. Set them aside and keep them warm. (Both carrots and leeks can be cooked at the same time as the partridges.)

7   Season the partridges. Cook them gently in a heavy iron
    casserole with 25g *(1 oz)* butter, the leeks, the livers and
    hearts from the giblets, the mirepoix and the sprig of
    thyme. Cook them for 20 minutes in all – 5 minutes on each
    side and 10 minutes on their backs. Two-thirds of the way
    through cooking, strain off the butter and replace it with
    75g *(2½ oz)* fresh butter. Baste the breasts of the birds with
    this butter several times during their last 5 minutes of
    cooking.

    When the partridges are done, cut them in half. Take out
    the bones that are easiest to detach from inside and keep
    the birds warm between two plates. Put the bones back into
    the casserole.

8   To make the gravy, put the casserole with the bones and
    cooking juices back on to the stove over a brisk heat.
    Deglaze with the champagne or white wine, and let it
    reduce. Add the game stock and let it simmer quite fast for
    2 minutes to extract all the flavour from the bones. Pass the
    gravy through a strainer.

Serving

9   Make a bed of leeks in the centre of each heated plate. Put
    one half partridge on top of each bed of leeks and arrange
    the carrots in a semi-circle around it. Coat the bird with the
    gravy.

Salad of Ptarmigan with Chicory and Ceps

Salade de perdrix des neiges aux endives et cèpes

The *perdrix blanche* of the Alps is now very rare; it could be replaced in this salad with partridges, or even pigeons.

Editor's note – In the British Isles the nearest equivalent of the *perdrix blanche* is the ptarmigan, which is not often available; however, grouse and capercaillies are near relations and may be used instead, as well as the partridges or pigeons suggested by Fredy Girardet.

For two people

2	ptarmigan *or* any of the alternatives suggested above
1	chicory
100g *(3½ oz)*	ceps *(Boletus edulis)*
2 tbsps	walnut oil
	white wine vinegar
½	lemon
1	large shallot
1–2	sprigs of thyme
	unsalted butter
	oil
	salt and pepper

Preparation

1 Remove the breasts from the birds (see page 121).

2 Remove the solid core at the heart of the chicory with a sharp kitchen knife, then cut the chicory lengthways into fine julienne strips.

3 Clean the ceps. Slice them finely using both caps and stems, if the latter are not wormy.

4 Make a vinaigrette with the 2 tablespoons of walnut oil, 1 tablespoon of the vinegar, the juice of the half lemon, salt and pepper.

5 Peel and finely chop the shallot.

Finishing

6 Season the julienne of chicory with the vinaigrette.

7   Season the breasts of the bird and gently cook them in a frying pan with a nut of butter and the thyme, so that they become a golden colour. This should take no more than 2 minutes, as you want the meat to stay pink. Remove the breasts and put them on a plate.

8   Make a drop of oil very hot in a clean frying pan. Add the sliced ceps and, when their liquid has evaporated, continue to cook them until they become a light golden colour. Add a little nut of butter and the chopped shallot. Let it colour slightly for a minute, then turn the contents of the pan on to a plate and sprinkle a dash of vinegar over them.

Serving

9   Serve this salad on individual heated plates. Arrange the chicory in a fan shape at the top, with the two breasts of each bird back to back in the centre and the little fricassée of ceps below.

Saddle of Hare in Strips with Pears
Râble de lièvre en aiguillettes aux poires Curé

The *poire Curé* which we use for this dish is very elongated. It is ready to use at Christmas after it has been ripened in the cellar.

Editor's note – The Conference or the Passe-Crassane are the nearest equivalents to the *poire Curé* in England.

For four people

1	saddle taken from a hare weighing 2kg *(4½ lb)*
2	pears (see notes above)
250ml *(scant ½ pint)*	red wine
1 tbsp	sugar
1	bay leaf
1	piece of cinnamon
3	peppercorns
	sauce poivrade (see page 252)
4 tbsps	*spätzli* (see page 198) for garnish (optional)
	unsalted butter
	oil
	salt and pepper

Preparation

1 Prepare the pears one day in advance, if possible, so that they have plenty of time to acquire a good deep colour. Peel them, halve them and remove the cores. Poach them in the red wine (reserving 2 tablespoons for the finishing step). Add the sugar, bay leaf, cinnamon and peppercorns. Simmer until the fruit is tender, with a piece of aluminium foil weighted down by a plate on top of them to keep them submerged. Keep them in the wine until you need them.

2 Make the base for *sauce poivrade.* Leave the finishing steps till later.

3 If you are having them, prepare the *spätzli.* Leave them in cold water until you are ready to serve the hare.

4 Remove the transparent skin from the saddle of hare.

Cooking and finishing

5 Reheat the pears in their wine, then drain them. Heat some butter in a frying pan and turn the pears in it on all sides. Add the 2 reserved tablespoons of red wine and let it reduce so that the pears become lightly glazed. Keep them warm.

6 To cook the saddle, pre-heat the oven to 280°C/530°F/ Gas 10. Season the saddle and first of all sear it all over in a frying pan with half a tablespoon of oil. Turn it on each side then put it into the pre-heated oven. Leave it there for 5–6 minutes, turning it so that both sides cook equally.

After 6 minutes, throw away the hot oil and replace it with a good-sized nut of butter. Turn the saddle on its back and make deep cuts along the fillets that lie on either side of the back-bone.

Finish the cooking with the oven door open and the saddle at the front of the oven, basting it constantly for 6–7 minutes. The meat should be bloody near the bone, but you can, if necessary, prolong this stage by a few minutes, still keeping the dish at the front of the oven.

7 Reheat the *sauce poivrade* and finish it (see page 252, steps 5 and 6).

8 If you are having the *spätzli*, drain them, dry them well, then toss them in some butter to finish them.

Serving

9 Take the fillets from the saddle with the help of a spoon and carve them on the slant. Divide the slices between four heated plates. Coat them lightly with the *sauce poivrade*. Garnish each plate with half a glazed pear and, if you are having them, 1 tablespoonful of *spätzli*.

Noisettes of Venison with Red Cabbage and Chestnuts

Noisettes de chevreuil poêlées au chou rouge et aux châtaignes

For four people

12	*noisettes* of venison, each weighing 50g *(1¾ oz)*
12	chestnuts
	oil
4	lumps of sugar
100ml *(scant ¼ pint)*	veal stock (see page 247)
2	pieces of celery, each measuring 3 × 5cm *(1⅜ × 2 in)*
600g *(1 lb 5 oz)*	red cabbage
1	large onion
1	apple
	unsalted butter
	red wine vinegar
150g *(5½ oz)*	mushrooms (use wild ones if they are in season)
1	small clove of garlic
1	small shallot
	salt and pepper

Preparation

1 The best and quickest way to peel and skin chestnuts is to score the brown, outer shells all over with a sharp knife, leaving only the light-coloured parts at the base of the chestnuts intact. Plunge them into a large pan of deep, boiling oil for a few moments. After this they can be peeled quite easily. The skin underneath comes off if you rub the shelled chestnuts in a cloth while they are still hot.

2 Put the four sugar lumps into a small, heavy saucepan and heat them until they melt and caramelise to a pale golden colour. Add 100ml *(scant ¼ pint)* water and the same quantity of veal stock. Stir to dissolve the caramel, then add the pieces of celery and the peeled chestnuts. Continue cooking, without too much stirring, until the chestnuts are soft and the liquid is syrupy. Take out the pieces of celery and set the pan aside.

3 Wash the red cabbage. Remove the outer leaves and the biggest ribs. Slice the leaves and the rest of the cabbage into strips of 0.5 × 3cm *(³⁄₁₆ × 1³⁄₈ in)*.

4 Peel and chop the onion. Peel and core the apple and slice it very finely.

5 Soften the onion in a little butter in a saucepan large enough to accommodate the cabbage. Add the cabbage and let it soften completely; this takes only a few minutes. Add a dash of vinegar and enough water to come barely half-way up the cabbage. Add the sliced apple, salt and pepper, then cover the pan and let the cabbage cook gently for about half an hour, or even a little less; this will depend on the quality of the cabbage.

6 Clean the mushrooms and, depending on their size, leave them whole, cut them in half or into quarters, or slice them.

7 Peel and chop the garlic and the shallot.

Finishing

8 Gently reheat the chestnuts and the red cabbage while you cook the mushrooms and the *noisettes* of venison.

9 To cook the mushrooms, make a dry, heavy iron frying pan very hot, then pour 1 tablespoon of oil into it. Add the mushrooms and cook them over a brisk heat. As they cook they will give out their juice. When this has evaporated, add 20g *(¾ oz)* butter, the chopped garlic and shallot, salt and pepper. Mix well and continue the cooking for a few moments more, until the contents have coloured nicely. Set the pan aside.

10 Season the *noisettes* with salt and pepper and fry them in a little very hot oil. Turn them over after 1 minute, add a good lump of butter and cook the second sides for exactly 1 minute more.

Serving

11 Serve on four heated plates, arranging three chestnuts on one side of each plate, a quarter of the red cabbage on the other and three *noisettes* in the centre. Divide the sautéed mushrooms into four and arrange them on top of the *noisettes.*

Vegetables
and Garnishes

Cooked Artichoke Hearts

Fonds d'artichauts (cuisson)

For four people

4 medium-sized violet artichokes
1 large onion
  dry white wine
  salt and pepper

Preparation

1 Shorten the artichoke stems to 4cm *(1½ in)*. Trim the leaves by one-third of their height.

2 Peel each artichoke, turning it on its axis as if you were peeling an orange, finishing with the stem trimmed to a point (the stems of violet artichokes are edible). As you work, squeeze lemon juice on to the artichokes to stop them discolouring. Peel the onion and slice it into rounds.

Cooking

3 Arrange the onion slices at the bottom of a saucepan. Put the prepared artichokes on top.

4 Pour in white wine to a depth of 1cm *(⅜ in)* and top up with water so that the liquid comes half-way up the sides of the artichokes. Season with salt and pepper. Cook at a simmer for half an hour.

Uses

Depending on the recipe, the artichokes can be cut into four or six sections and kept cold or reheated in a little of their own cooking liquid.

Charlotte of Aubergine and Courgettes with Chicken Liver

Charlotte d'aubergines et courgettes aux foie de volaille

Editor's note – If you like, you can use the courgette skins as well as the aubergine skins to line the moulds. Prepare them in the same way, so that some of the charlottes are black (aubergine), some green (courgette) and some striped (alternative strips of aubergine and courgette).

For four people

2	large aubergines
150g *(5½ oz)*	courgettes
100g *(3½ oz)*	chicken livers and chicken hearts
4	new-season onions
4	cloves of garlic
	unsalted butter
	olive oil
1	sprig of parsley
	salt and pepper

Preparation

1 Using a potato peeler, peel the skin off the aubergines in broad, fine bands. Blanch the skins for 30 seconds in boiling water, then drain them. Melt a little nut of butter in a frying pan and quickly coat the strips of aubergine with it by laying them in the pan for a few seconds.

2 Using a brush, paint some softened butter inside four moulds 6cm *(2⅜ in)* in diameter and 4cm *(1½ in)* high. Line them with the strips of aubergine skin so that when the moulds are turned out the dark sides of the skin are on the outside. Arrange the strips to radiate from the centre of the moulds and to overlap the tops by 3cm *(1⅜ in)*. Fill the centre space with a rectangle of skin.

3 Peel the courgettes (see editor's note above). Cut tiny dice, 3mm *(⅛ in)* square, from 125g *(4½ oz)* peeled courgettes. Cut the same size and weight of dice from the peeled aubergines (there will be some aubergine left over for another use).

4 Chop the onions and garlic fairly coarsely.

5 Starting with a cold frying pan, heat the onions and garlic with 1½ tablespoons of olive oil. Let them sweat without colouring for 3 minutes, just long enough to soften them. Add the diced aubergines and courgettes with another tablespoon of olive oil. Season with salt and pepper and sauté for 3 minutes. Remove the pan from the heat and set it aside.

6 Chop the chicken hearts and livers coarsely. Season them with salt and pepper and add them to the vegetables.

7 Chop the parsley very finely and add a big pinch of it to the mixture.

8 Fill the moulds with the mixture, pressing it down well with the back of a spoon. Fold the aubergine skin back over the top of the mixture. Press with the palm of your hand to firm down the filling.

Cooking

9 Pre-heat the oven to 250°C/480°F/Gas 9. Arrange the moulds in a bain-marie, with water up to one-third of their height. Bring it to the boil on top of the stove, then place the bain-marie in the pre-heated oven for 20 minutes.

Serving

10 Take the charlottes out of their moulds while they are still warm. They can be eaten on their own as a first course or they can accompany a meat dish such as lamb.

Stewed Red Cabbage

Emincé de chou rouge

For four people

600g *(1 lb 5 oz)*	red cabbage
1	apple
1	large onion
40g *(1¼ oz)*	unsalted butter
	red wine vinegar
	salt and pepper

Preparation and cooking

1   Clean and trim the cabbage, removing the central core and the outer leaves. Trim the largest ribs from the rest and cut the usable parts of the cabbage into 3 × 0.5cm *(1⅜ × ³⁄₁₆ in)* strips.

2   Peel the apple and the onion. Chop both very finely but keep them separate.

3   Melt the butter in a heavy iron pan on a moderate heat. Add the chopped onion. Let it soften for a few moments, then add the cabbage.

4   Stir for a few moments, until the cabbage has softened a little, then add a dash of red wine vinegar and a little water. This should come to a depth of half the height of the cabbage.

5   Add the apple, salt and pepper, and cover the pan. Leave it to cook gently for about half an hour. Set it aside until you are ready to serve it.

Finishing and serving

6   Reheat the cabbage gently before serving. Serve it with the *noisettes* of venison on page 172 or other game.

Green Cabbage

Chou vert en légume

Editor's note – Fredy Girardet's use of only the large leaves of a cabbage may seem extravagant, but he does it to provide pieces of a uniform size and texture. The smallest inner leaves are not wasted – they are chopped finely and used in terrines.

The leaves are easier to detach if you first cut the large conical core out of the cabbage.

Another recipe for cabbage will be found in the recipe for Pot-au-Feu of Pigeon (see page 138).

For four people

20	leaves from a savoy cabbage
6	thin rashers of smoked bacon
2	new-season onions
50g *(1¾ oz)*	unsalted butter
	salt and pepper

Preparation

1 Choose the largest leaves from an already trimmed cabbage. Trim out the main, central ribs. Blanch the leaves for 1 minute in a big pan of boiling salted water. Drain the water off and refresh the leaves in cold water. Drain them again and lay them flat on a tea-towel. Pat them thoroughly dry with another tea-towel.

2 Cut the bacon into very narrow julienne strips, 2mm *(⅛ in)* wide. Chop the onions finely.

Finishing

3 Cut each blanched and dried cabbage leaf into four or five pieces.

4 Put two large lumps of butter into a large frying pan on a low heat with the strips of bacon and the chopped onion.

5 As soon as the butter foams, add the cabbage. Add salt and pepper, mix well and leave the pan to simmer over a gentle heat for 8–10 minutes, just long enough to heat the cabbage through and to allow it to give out some of its own moisture.

Serving

6 Serve this cabbage with Pigeon with Cabbage (see page 140).

Glazed Carrots
Carrottes glacées

For four people

800g *(1¾ lb)*	carrots
2	medium-sized onions
50g *(1¾ oz)*	unsalted butter
	salt and pepper

Preparation

1 Peel the carrots and cut them into rounds, on the slant. Peel and chop the onions.

Cooking and finishing

2 Soften the chopped onions in the butter in a saucepan. When the onions are soft but not coloured, add the carrots. Season them, stir them well to mix the onions and carrots, and let them colour slightly before adding water to a depth of half their height.

3 Cover the pan and leave it to cook gently for 20 minutes.

Serving

4 These carrots accompany the casseroled partridge on page 167. They are suitable for any similar meat or game dishes.

Glazed Wild Chestnuts

Châtaignes fondantes

Editor's note – *Châtaignes* are small wild chestnuts. The cultivated *marrons*, which are usually on sale in England, are larger, so reduce the quantity if you are using this kind.

For four people

20	wild chestnuts (see editor's note above)
6	lumps of sugar
150ml *(¼ pint)*	water
150ml *(¼ pint)*	veal stock (see page 247)
3	pieces of celery, measuring about 5 × 3cm *(2 × 1⅜ in)*
	salt and pepper

Preparation

1 Peel and skin the chestnuts (see page 173, step 1).

Cooking

2 Put the sugar lumps in a saucepan on a low heat; the sugar will melt, then become a pale caramel. Add the water and veal stock immediately and stir to dissolve the caramel (which will have hardened instantly). Add the pieces of celery and the chestnuts and continue cooking, gently and without stirring too much, until the liquid becomes syrupy. At the same time, the chestnuts should be soft. Take out the pieces of celery and set the pan aside.

Finishing

3 Reheat the chestnuts gently before serving.

Serving

4 These chestnuts are served with the *noisettes* of venison on page 172. They are good with any game, furred or feathered.

Swiss Chard

Bette

For two people

4	large Swiss chard leaves, with stems
	olive oil
	a pinch of thyme
40g *(1½ oz)*	unsalted butter
3 tbsps	double cream
	salt and pepper

Preparation

1 Wash the chard leaves. Cut off the green parts and cut them into three or four pieces, removing the largest veins. String the central stems and cut them into thin slices 5mm *(³⁄₁₆ in)* wide.

2 Blanch the leafy parts in boiling salted water for 3 minutes. Drain them and dry them on a cloth.

Finishing

3 Put the sliced chard stems into a frying pan with a few drops of olive oil and a pinch of thyme. Do not cook them for more than 6 minutes, as the pieces must remain firm. Season them with salt and pepper and add half the butter at the end of their cooking time.

4 Roughly chop the blanched and dried leaves. Put them into a saucepan with the rest of the butter and let them soften over a medium heat. Season with salt and pepper and add the cream. Cook gently for a few moments more until the sauce thickens.

Serving

5 Arrange the leaves in the centre of a plate with the stems in a ring around them. Swiss chard accompanies the sautéed fillet of veal on page 152.

Fricassée of Ceps

Fricassée de cèpes

For four people

600g *(1 lb 5 oz)*	ceps *(Boletus edulis)*
1	clove of garlic
4	shallots
	oil
50g *(1¾ oz)*	unsalted butter
	salt and pepper

Preparation

1 Clean the mushrooms, removing any worm-eaten stems. Slice the rest finely. Peel and chop the garlic and shallots finely.

Finishing

2 Make a drop or two of oil very hot in a frying pan and add the ceps. They will exude juice at first, but continue cooking until it has all evaporated, then add the butter, garlic and shallots. Season with salt and pepper. Cook gently for 1 minute, then take the pan off the heat and serve.

Serving

3 These ceps form an integral part of the warm salad of ptarmigan or partridge breasts on page 169 and the *noisettes* of venison on page 172. Other wild mushrooms and cultivated mushrooms can be cooked and served in the same way.

Chicory with Lemon

Endives au citron

Editor's note – Lime juice can be used instead of lemon juice in this recipe, especially if it is to accompany fish.

For four people

1kg *(2¼ lb)*	chicory
3 tbsps	lemon juice
15g *(½ oz)*	sugar
40g *(1¼ oz)*	unsalted butter
	salt and pepper

Preparation

1 Carefully wipe the chicory. Remove any damaged outer leaves.

2 Cut them on the slant, holding the *chicons* in one hand while you make slices about 15mm *(½ in)* thick, but with each cut give the *chicon* a quarter-turn so that the slices become wedge-shaped.

3 Separate the pieces and leave them in a salad bowl.

Finishing

4 Just before cooking, season the chicory pieces with the sugar, 3 pinches of salt and 10 turns of the pepper-mill. Add the lemon juice and mix everything together carefully with your hands.

5 Using two non-stick frying pans, heat half the butter in one and half in the other. Divide the chicory between the two and cook over a high heat for 3 minutes – no longer, or it will become sad and limp: this is why you must use two pans. (It is impossible to cook more than 500g *(1 lb)* chicory in one pan, however large the pan may be.)

Serving

6 Chicory cooked in this way makes an excellent accompaniment to scallops (see page 107), partridge (see page 169) and chicken (see page 125).

Leeks 'Vaudoise'

Poireaux à la Vaudoise

For four people

4	leeks
50g *(1¾ oz)*	unsalted butter
100ml *(scant ¼ pint)*	double cream
	salt and pepper

Preparation

1 Trim the dark green parts from the leeks, keeping only the paler green and the white parts. Remove any damaged outer leaves. Wash the leeks and cut them into four lengthways, and then into pieces 1cm *(⅜ in)* across. Separate all the pieces.

Finishing

2 Heat 30g *(1 oz)* of the butter in a saucepan. Add the leeks and cook them briskly for 2 minutes. Add 100ml *(a scant ¼ pint)* water and continue to cook, still over a brisk heat, until all the water has evaporated.

3 Add the cream and cook for another minute, stirring all the time, still over a good heat. Season, and remove the pan from the heat as soon as the leeks are well coated with the cream. Add 20g *(¾ oz)* butter and keep them warm.

Serving

4 Make a bed of these leeks for the *matelote* of sole and *langoustines* on page 90, or the breast of chicken on page 121, or use them as part of a *feuilleté* filling, as in the recipe on page 58.

Onion Confit

Oignons confits

For four to six people

600g *(14 oz)*	onions
500ml *(1 pint)*	good red wine
100ml *(scant ¼ pint)*	red wine vinegar
70g *(2½ oz)*	honey
40g *(1¼ oz)*	unsalted butter
	salt and pepper

Preparation and cooking

1   Peel and slice the onions. Put them into a saucepan with the wine vinegar and the wine, so that they are just covered by the liquid. Cook them over a low heat until all the liquid is absorbed; this should take about half to three-quarters of an hour.

2   Next, add 500ml *(1 pint)* water. Continue cooking, still over a low heat, for about half an hour. Stir from time to time to make sure the *confit* is not sticking to the bottom of the pan. When it is completely soft, the *confit* is cooked.

3   Add the butter, honey, salt and pepper. Stir well and set the pan aside until you are ready to serve.

Finishing

4   Reheat the *confit* gently. Taste again for seasoning and sharpen it a little by adding a dash of vinegar.

Serving

5   This *confit* is served warm; it is given as an accompaniment to the John Dory on page 73. It would also go well with meat or game.

A Paillasson of Potatoes
Paillasson de pommes de terre

The celebrated Swiss *rösti* is similar to this dish, but here the potatoes are fried without pre-cooking, whereas for a *rösti* they are parboiled, in their skins, then peeled, cooled and grated before being fried in a cake.

Editor's note – A *paillasson* is a thin straw mat, which this dish resembles exactly. Cook it in a large pan or in two smaller ones; if the 'mat' is too thick, it will be raw in the middle and burnt outside.

For four people

8 medium-sized floury potatoes
   oil
   salt and pepper

Preparation

1 Grate the potatoes into thin julienne strips, similar to the size used for *céleri rémoulade.* You can use a food processor, but an ordinary grater or a mandoline makes better shreds. If the strips are very moist, put them in a cloth and dry them a little.

Finishing

2 Heat a little oil in a large non-stick pan. When it is very hot, throw in the potatoes. Season them and stir to begin with, then let them mat together and form a crust underneath. As soon as the underside is crisp turn the 'mat' over and continue cooking until the second side is also crisp. The cooking time should be as swift and brief as possible.

Serving

3 Serve immediately. The *paillasson* is recommended as an accompaniment to the saddle of rabbit on page 143 and is especially good with game.

Lyonnaise Potatoes

Pommes Lyonnaise

Editor's note – This dish is simple enough as long as your frying pan is very large, the oil is very hot and the potatoes are cooked in one layer only.

For four people

500g *(1 lb 2 oz)*   new potatoes
100g *(3½ oz)*   onions
2 tbsps   oil
   salt and pepper

Preparation

1 Peel the potatoes and slice them finely – 2mm *(1/16 in)* thick – with a mandoline. A food processor will do as well, as long as the slices are thin.

2 Peel the onions. Slice them finely too, and separate the rings in each slice.

Finishing

3 Heat the oil in a large frying pan.

4 Season the potatoes and onions.

5 Put the slices of potato into the pan first and sauté them quickly, turning them over several times, for 2 minutes. Add the onions and continue cooking, still stirring and turning, for 3–4 minutes more, until both potatoes and onions are crisp and golden.

Serving

6 These potatoes are made into a bed for the *noisettes* of lamb on page 155.

Purée of New Potatoes with Olive Oil

Purée de pommes nouvelles à l'huile d'olive

Editor's note – You may need less oil than the amount given below; some kinds of potato absorb it more readily than others. If the oil starts to come out of the potato after you have mixed it in, you have added too much.

For four people

300g *(10½ oz)*   new potatoes, peeled or scraped
120ml *(¼ pint)*   double cream
120ml *(¼ pint)*   fruity olive oil
salt, pepper and cayenne

Cooking and finishing

1   Cook the peeled potatoes in boiling salted water. Drain them and make them into a purée, using either a sieve or a *mouli-légumes.* Warm the cream.

2   Put the purée into a saucepan. Add the warmed cream and beat until all the cream is absorbed into the potato.

3   With the pan still on the heat, add the oil, mixing it in with a wooden spoon. Beat the mixture for a minute or two after all the oil has been absorbed. Season with salt, pepper and cayenne.

Serving

4   Serve this purée with fish, shellfish or any dish which is redolent of the south of France.

Gratin of Potatoes Girardet

Gratin de pommes de terre Girardet

The gratin is best if it is given gentle, slow cooking.

For four people

400g *(14 oz)*	floury potatoes
1	small clove of garlic
200ml *(scant ½ pint)*	milk
100ml *(scant ¼ pint)*	double cream
20g *(¾ oz)*	unsalted butter
	salt, pepper, cayenne and nutmeg

Preparation

1 Peel the potatoes and cut them into thin slices about 3mm *(⅛ in)* thick. Above all, do not wash them.

2 Peel and chop the clove of garlic very finely and mix it with the slices of potato.

3 Put the potatoes into a saucepan with just enough milk to cover them. Season with salt, pepper, cayenne and a few gratings of nutmeg.

4 Put the pan over a fairly high heat and cook the potatoes for 4–5 minutes, or until you can see that the milk has blended and thickened a little with the starch given out by the potatoes. At this point, add half the cream and just bring the pan to the boil. Take it off the stove and taste for seasoning.

5 Butter a gratin dish. This should be big enough to take the potatoes in a layer not more than 2cm *(¾ in)* thick. Arrange the potatoes in the dish with their creamy milk. Add the rest of the cream and mix it in well. Sprinkle a few flakes of butter on the surface.

Cooking

6 Pre-heat the oven to 160°C/320°F/Gas 3. Bake the gratin at the bottom of the oven for a good 1½ hours.

Serving

7 This rich, creamy potato dish is excellent with any plainly cooked poultry or roast meat.

Gnocchi à la Piedmontaise

Gnocchi à la piémontaise

I like these best lightly tossed and browned in butter after cooking.

For four people

300g *(10½ oz)*	floury potatoes
100g *(3½ oz)*	plain flour
1	egg yolk
2 heaped tbsps	green herbs (such as basil, parsley and chervil), chopped
	olive oil
	salt, pepper and grated nutmeg

Preparation

1   Boil the potatoes in their skins in salted water until they are completely tender.

2   Peel them while they are still hot and purée them immediately in a *mouli-légumes* or potato masher. Pile the purée on to a floured board so that you can make a well in the heap of purée. Leave it to cool, then season it with salt, pepper and a little grated nutmeg. Sprinkle all these seasonings on the top of the heap and finally pour a little thread of olive oil all over the purée.

3   When the purée is really cool, put the flour in the centre of the well. Mix the chopped herbs lightly into the egg yolk with a fork and add this mixture to the flour. Working as quickly and lightly as you can, incorporate the egg, flour and potato with your fingertips until it is well mixed, then quickly press the dough together with the heel of your hand as if you were making *pâte brisée*. Leave it to rest for 10 minutes.

4   Flour the table top or a pastry board. Cut the dough in half and make two long rolls about 2cm *(¾ in)* thick. Cut them into pieces 1cm *(⅜ in)* wide. If you like, roll each piece over the convex side of a fork to make little grooved *gnocchi*, but this is optional, as it is purely for decoration.

Cooking

5   Poach the *gnocchi* in well-salted boiling water. After they rise to the surface, give them a moment or two of cooking to soften and swell, then scoop them out and drain them. Keep them warm.

Serving

6   The *gnocchi* can be served with a herb-flavoured tomato sauce, or they can be sautéed in a frying pan, well browned and served sprinkled with Parmesan. They can also be smothered in cream and gratinéed under a grill.

Parsley as a Vegetable

Persil en légume

For four people

600g *(14 oz)*	curled parsley, stripped of all its stalks
1	large shallot
60g *(2¼ oz)*	unsalted butter
200ml *(scant ½ pint)*	double cream
	salt and pepper

Preparation

1   Bring a large pan of salted water to the boil. Put the well-trimmed parsley in it and cook it for 6 minutes after the water returns to the boil. Drain and dry the parsley thoroughly with a tea-towel.

2   Peel and chop the shallot finely.

Finishing

3   Put the shallot into a frying pan with the butter over a medium heat. As soon as the butter froths, add the well-dried parsley and stir it about with a fork. Add the cream. Let it bubble up twice so that the cream thickens slightly and some of it is absorbed by the parsley. Season with salt and pepper and remove the pan from the heat.

Serving

4 This is suggested as an accompaniment to the *mignonnette* of lamb on page 154. It would go well with any similar meat, and also with grilled fish.

Pears in Red Wine
Poires au vin rouge

Editor's note – These pears are intended not as a cold dessert but as a hot garnish to dishes like the saddle of hare on page 170.

For four people

4	pears
400ml approx. *(⅔ pint)*	red wine
2 tbsps	sugar
1	small piece of cinnamon stick
1	bay leaf
6	peppercorns
30g *(1 oz)*	unsalted butter

Preparation

1 One day in advance, peel the pears, cut them in two and core them.

2 Put the pears closely side by side in a saucepan. Cover them with the red wine, reserving 3 tablespoons for the finish. Add the sugar, cinnamon, bay leaf and peppercorns.

3 Cover the pears with a sheet of aluminium foil under an upturned plate to keep them completely immersed in the wine while they cook and simmer them until they are tender.

4 When the pears are tender, take the pan off the stove and leave them to macerate until the following day so that they become a good dark red colour.

Finishing

5 Reheat the pears in their juice, then drain them.

6 Melt the butter in a frying pan and add the pears. Lightly baste them, without cooking them. Add the 3 reserved tablespoons of uncooked red wine. Let it reduce and thicken so that it lightly glazes the pears.

Serving

7 Serve the pears hot as a garnish (one half per person).

Confit of Black Radish

Radis noirs confits

Depending on whether the radishes are to be a garnish to game or not, use game stock or veal stock.

For four people

1kg *(2¼ lb)*	black radishes
50g *(1¾ oz)*	butter
100ml *(scant ¼ pint)*	game *or* veal stock (see pages 248 and 247)
100ml *(scant ¼ pint)*	white port (see editor's note, page 9)
100ml *(scant ¼ pint)*	dry white wine
	lemon juice
	salt and pepper

Preparation

1 Quarter the radishes then, with a little knife, shape them like large cloves of garlic, peeling them as you do so.

2 Heat the butter in a saucepan and cook the radishes gently for 5–6 minutes. Drain off the cooking butter.

3   Add the veal stock, port and wine. Season with salt and pepper and let the radishes cook for just under a quarter of an hour, until they are tender and the liquid is syrupy. If the syrup is too thick, add a little water – but not too much, as there should be not more than 2 tablespoons of juice per person left at the end. Adjust the seasoning and add a dash of lemon juice. Set the pan aside until you are ready to serve.

Finishing

4   Gently reheat the *confit*.

Serving

5   Serve warm, sprinkled with freshly crushed black pepper *(mignonnette)*. The *confit* makes an accompaniment to pheasant (see page 165), or other game, or roast lamb.

Sautéed Salsifies

Salsifis sautés

For four people

8	salsifies
2 tbsps	oil
30g *(1 oz)*	unsalted butter
	salt and pepper

Preparation

1   Peel the salsifies. Remove the ends, then cut the peeled roots into little sticks 3cm *(1⅜ in)* long and 5mm *(³⁄₁₆ in)* square.

Cooking and finishing

2   Heat 2 tablespoons of oil in a frying pan. Add the little
    salsify sticks and stir them over a high heat for 2–3 minutes.
    Lower the heat as they begin to brown and continue
    cooking for 5 minutes, tossing the pan to turn them from
    time to time.

3   Season with salt and pepper. Add the butter. Continue
    cooking until the salsify has had about 12–15 minutes of
    cooking in all.

Serving

4   These salsifies are given as an accompaniment to the roast
    duck on page 131. They would go well with any roast
    poultry.

Spätzli
Spätzli

Spätzli are a typical Swiss dish and, like *gnocchi*, they often lend an
agreeably rustic note to a meal.

For four to six people

5	eggs
250g *(9 oz)*	plain flour
150ml *(¼ pint)*	milk
	unsalted butter
	oil
	salt, pepper and grated nutmeg

Preparation

1   Beat the eggs into the flour until you have a smooth, thick,
    homogenous mixture.

2   Thin the mixture by gradually adding the milk, beating it as
    you do so. Season with salt, pepper and nutmeg, mixing
    them in carefully.

3   Bring a large pan of salted water to the boil.

4   Hold a special *spätzli*-maker, or a colander-like strainer with holes 1cm *(⅜ in)* in diameter, over the boiling water and scrape the *spätzli* mixture through the holes. Use a plastic pastry-scraper or *corne* to do this. The *spätzli* will fall into the water in little balls. Make a few at a time.

5   As the *spätzli* rise to the surface, remove them with a skimmer and throw them into a basin of cold water.

6   When they are all cooked, drain them, giving them plenty of time to do so. Add a tablespoonful of oil to prevent them from sticking to one another.

Finishing

7   Just before you are ready to serve, fry them in butter until they are nicely golden and season them.

8   Serve *spätzli* as an accompaniment to game, ragoûts and sautés.

Baby Turnips with Green Topknots
Navets nouveaux en tige

For four people

32   baby turnips, with their green stems
      unsalted butter
      salt and pepper

Preparation

1   Shorten the green stems of the turnips to 6cm *(2⅜ in)* and peel them by turning each one like an apple.

2   Protect the stems by wrapping each topknot in aluminium foil. Cook the turnips in boiling salted water for 7–10 minutes – the length of time depends on the freshness of the vegetables. Drain them and let them cool.

3   Remove the aluminium foil and cut each little turnip (and its topknot) into four quarters.

4   Butter an oven dish. Arrange the turnip quarters in it. Season them with salt and pepper and dot each one with a flake of butter. They can be kept waiting like this until just before serving.

Finishing

5   Slide the dish of turnips into a very hot oven for 5 minutes to reheat them.

Serving

6   The turnips are decorative enough to be arranged in a double circle on each plate, with their little topknots pointing outwards. They accompany the guinea fowl on page 129, and are also very good with lamb.

Cold Desserts

Bananas
with Lime and Orange Zest
Bananes aux zestes de citron vert et orange

For four people

4	bananas
120g *(4 oz)*	sugar
½	orange
½	lime

Preparation

1 Three hours in advance, make a syrup by dissolving the sugar in 200ml *(a scant ½ pint)* water over a medium heat then simmer for 5–6 minutes.

2 Pare the zests (the very outermost skins) from the lime and orange, and cut them into the finest julienne strips.

3 Press the juice from the lime and orange.

4 Slice the bananas into rounds.

5 Add the fruit juices and their zests to the syrup, reserving a few zests for decoration. Add the bananas to the syrup, then pour everything into a fruit dish. Sprinkle the reserved zests on top and leave the fruit to macerate in a cool place for at least 3 hours.

Serving

6 Serve the bananas in a pretty fruit dish as part of a group of other cold fruit desserts. You will find more recipes on pages 204–7.

Cocktail of Little Fruits with Cassis

Cocktail de petits fruits au cassis

This dish is a harmony of sharp tastes that is very refreshing.

For four people

200g *(7 oz)*	gooseberries
200g *(7 oz)*	redcurrants
200g *(7 oz)*	blackcurrants
	juice of 1 lemon
3 tbsps	crème de cassis
100g *(3½ oz)*	sugar

Preparation

1 Several hours in advance, wash all the fruit. Remove tops, tails and stalks where necessary.

2 Cut each of the gooseberries in half.

3 Mix all the ingredients together and leave them to macerate for several hours in a cool place.

Serving

4 Serve the 'cocktail' in a pretty fruit dish as part of a group of other cold fruit desserts. You will find more recipes below and on pages 203, 205, 206 and 207.

Kiwis with Passion Fruit Juice

Kiwis au jus de fruits de la passion

Editor's note – To obtain enough of the passion fruit juice that is essential for this recipe you will need to crush at least eight passion fruits. Pure, commercial passion fruit juice would do, but it is difficult to find. Juice sold as 'passion fruit' nearly always contains 50 per cent juice from other fruits, which spoils its true flavour. If you need to top up the quantity of juice with any other fruit juice, use orange.

For four to six people

6	kiwi fruits
100ml *(very scant ¼ pint)*	passion fruit juice
	sugar

Preparation

1 At least 3 hours in advance, peel and slice the kiwi fruits and arrange them neatly in a pretty fruit dish that can resist boiling liquid.

2 Put the passion fruit juice into a little saucepan. Add sugar to taste and bring it just to the boil. Pour it hot over the kiwis. Leave the fruit to macerate for at least 3 hours in a cold place.

Serving

3 Serve the kiwis in their fruit dish along with a selection of other cold fruit desserts. You will find recipes below and on pages 203, 204, 206 and 207.

Kumquat Confit
Kumquats confits

You can serve these kumquats alone, or as an accompaniment to the chocolate sorbet on page 213. They could also form part of the choice of cold fruit desserts on pages 203, 204, 206 and 207.

For eight people

1.5kg *(3½ lb)*   kumquats
1 litre *(1¾ pints)*   water
500g *(1 lb 2 oz)*   sugar

Preparation

1 One or two hours in advance, cut the kumquats into four lengthways, and remove the pips.

2 Put the kumquats into a saucepan with the water and sugar and let them cook very gently, uncovered, for half an hour.

Finishing and serving

3 Leave the kumquats in a pretty fruit dish to cool for an hour or two and serve them in the dish (see note above).

Apples in Red Wine
Pommes au vin rouge

Editor's note – Fredy Girardet uses Reinette or Maygold apples. The nearest British equivalent would be Blenheim Orange or James Grieves in autumn, and Newton Wonder or Golden Delicious later on. You need an apple that will hold its shape during cooking.

For four people

1kg *(2¼ lb)*	apples (see editor's note above)
500ml *(1 pint)*	red wine
1	stick of cinnamon
250g *(9 oz)*	sugar

Preparation

1 Ten hours in advance, cook the wine, cinnamon and sugar over a brisk heat for 10 minutes, using a broad, shallow saucepan.

2 Peel the apples and, using a melon-baller of about 2.5cm *(1 in)* diameter, cut them into little balls.

3 Throw the apple-balls into the hot wine. They should not overlap: this is why you need a broad, shallow pan. Simmer them for 5–7 minutes, covered with aluminium foil to keep them submerged.

4 When the apples are cooked but still firm, remove the pan from the stove. Let the apple-balls macerate in the red wine for about 10 hours to take on a good red colour.

Serving

5 Serve these apples, well chilled, with a scoop of Vanilla Ice-cream (see page 211), or include them in a selection of cold fruit desserts. You will find more recipes on pages 203, 204, 205 and 207.

Oriental Oranges

Oranges à l'orientale

This is an adaptation of an old recipe. It was traditionally made with whole oranges peeled down to the flesh ... but the skin left between the segments always spoiled it.

For eight people

12	large oranges
200g *(7 oz)*	sugar
3 tbsps	Grand Marnier *or* Cointreau
2 tbsps	grenadine syrup

Preparation

1 Peel the zest from the oranges in long strips, taking as little of the pith as possible.

2 Cut the zest into very, very fine julienne strips.

3 Next, remove the pith in vertical strips to expose the flesh of the oranges. Then, holding the oranges over a strainer with a bowl beneath to catch all the juice, cut each segment away from the membranes that divide one from another, and from the central core of pith.

4 Squeeze all the discarded membranes to extract every drop of juice, if any flesh remains on them, and add it to the already collected juice.

5 Blanch the julienned zest in boiling water for 1 minute. Refresh in cold water and drain in a sieve.

Cooking

6 Put the sugar into a large, wide saucepan and cook over a moderate, steady heat until the sugar melts and becomes a light golden colour.

7 Add the collected orange juice and, stirring to mix well, cook until the liquid has the consistency of a light syrup.

8 Add the julienned zest to the syrup, as well as the liqueur and the grenadine syrup. If a scum forms, remove it with a spoon as if you were making jam. Bring it briefly to the boil.

9   Add the orange segments and shake the pan well so that they all absorb the syrup. They should be hot, but they should not be allowed to cook. Set the pan aside.

At this point, if you like, you can add another drop of liqueur to the pan after you have taken it off the heat; this strengthens the flavour.

Serving

10   Arrange the segments on four plates to look like stars. Coat them with the syrup and decorate them with the julienned zests.

Alternatively, serve the oranges in a fruit dish, with a selection of some of the other cold fruit desserts given on pages 203, 204, 205 and 206.

Wild Strawberry Mousse

Mousse de fraises des bois

This is almost as refreshing as a sorbet.

For four people

280g *(10 oz)*	wild strawberries
100g *(3½ oz)*	sugar
160ml *(good ¼ pint)*	champagne
	lemon juice

Preparation

1   At least half an hour in advance, clean the strawberries. Reserve 85g *(3 oz)* and lightly sprinkle them with a little of the sugar and a drop or two of lemon juice.

2   Liquidise the rest of the strawberries with the rest of the sugar and all but 4 tablespoons of the champagne. Add a little lemon juice.

3 Frost four cocktail glasses by lightly moistening their rims with lemon juice to a depth of about 5mm (³⁄₁₆ in), then dip them into caster sugar. Do not overdo it or they will not look so pretty.

Finishing and serving

4 Put 20g (¾ oz) of the whole, sugared strawberries into each glass with a tablespoon of champagne. Top up with the mousse. Leave the glasses in the freezer for half an hour before serving.

Caramel Ice-cream

Glace au caramel

This is a classic recipe. The important moment comes when the sugar has caramelised to the point where it is brown but has not yet become bitter. Then, and only then, add the cream.

Editor's note – The caramel makes a very heavy mixture. Take care not to over-tax your ice-cream machine.

To make 1 litre (1¾ pints)

2	vanilla pods
250g (9 oz)	lump sugar
200ml (scant ½ pint)	double cream
350ml (just over ½ pint)	milk
8	egg yolks

Preparation and cooking

1 Split each vanilla pod and break both into three pieces. Put them with the sugar lumps in a heat-proof earthenware pot or an enamelled cast-iron pan and set it over a gentle heat.

2 When the sugar begins to melt and colour, stir with a wooden spatula until it becomes a beautiful brown caramel. Never increase the heat: this is the secret of success.

3 When the caramel is exactly right (see note above), take the pot or pan off the heat and add the cream. Watch out for splashes and splutters.

4 Return the pot to the stove and stir with a spatula until the caramel has completely dissolved in the cream. Remove from the heat.

5 Put the milk in a saucepan and bring it to the boil.

6 Beat the egg yolks with a fork in a basin.

7 Pour the milk slowly on to the egg yolks. Whisk vigorously at the same time to avoid cooking the yolks.

8 Incorporate the egg-and-milk mixture into the caramel, while whisking, to make a caramel custard.

9 Put the completed mixture on the heat and whisk until it shows the first signs of boiling.

10 Remove the pan from the stove. Take out the vanilla pieces and strain the custard through a *chinois*. Leave it to cool.

Finishing

11 Pour the mixture into a *sorbetière* and churn according to the manufacturer's instructions until the ice-cream is made.

Variation

Crush or chop 70g *(2½ oz)* praline (see page 259) and add it to the cool ice-cream mixture. Put the mixture in a *sorbetière* and churn according to the manufacturer's instructions. The crunchiness of the praline and the smoothness of the ice-cream form an agreeable contrast in the mouth.

Vanilla Ice-cream

Glace à la vanille

To make 1.5 litres *(2½ pints)*

2	vanilla pods
250g *(9 oz)*	sugar
6	egg yolks
500ml *(1 pint)*	milk
600ml *(just over 1 pint)*	double cream

Preparation

1 Open the vanilla pods and scrape out all the little seeds with the flat of a knife.

2 Mix the vanilla seeds on a board with 1 tablespoon of the sugar, making sure the seeds are well distributed so that later on they are not all found sticking together in little groups in the ice-cream. Crush them a little with the flat of a knife.

3 Mix the prepared sugar with the rest of the sugar in a bowl. Add the egg yolks and beat the mixture until it lightens in colour.

4 Pour the milk into a saucepan. Add the empty vanilla pods and bring it to the boil.

5 Pour the boiling milk on to the egg-and-sugar mixture, whisking fast. Remove the vanilla pods.

6 Put the mixture into a saucepan and heat it gently, stirring all the time, until it thickens just enough to coat a wooden spatula or spoon. (This is now technically a custard.)

7 Add the cream. Take the pan off the heat and let the custard cool completely.

Finishing

8 Pour the mixture into a *sorbetière* and churn according to the manufacturer's instructions until the ice-cream is made.

Serving

9 If you like, accompany this ice-cream with Apples in Red Wine (see page 206).

Three Citrus Fruit Sorbets

Les trois sorbets aux agrumes

Except for the lime sorbet, to which water must be added because limes are so powerfully sour, these sorbets are really iced fruit juices which measure no more than 15–16° on the hydrometer. They are best eaten as soon as they have been made.

Each recipe makes just over 1 litre *(1¾–2 pints)*

Lime sorbet
500ml *(1 pint)* lime juice
finely grated zest of 1 lime
400g *(14 oz)* sugar

Blood-orange sorbet
1 litre *(1¾ pints)* blood-orange juice
300–350g *(10½–12 oz)* sugar (depending on the sourness of the oranges)

Grapefruit sorbet
1 litre *(1¾ pints)* grapefruit juice
300g *(10½ oz)* sugar

Preparation

In each case, having squeezed out the juices, dissolve the sugar by stirring it into the juice, then make the sorbet in a *sorbetière* in the usual way.

For the lime sorbet, simply add the grated zest before you put the juice into the *sorbetière*.

Serving

Serve a scoop of each sorbet on previously chilled, ice-cold plates or dishes.

Apple Sorbet

Sorbet à la pomme

Sharp, juicy apples are best for this recipe.

To make 1 litre *(1¾ pints)*

4	large apples
300ml *(½ pint)*	apple juice
200g *(7 oz)*	sugar
	juice of ½ lemon

Preparation

1 Cook the apples, peeled and cut into quarters, with the apple juice and sugar.

2 Put it all into a food processor or liquidiser to make a very fine purée.

3 Add the lemon juice, then strain the purée through a fine *chinois* or conical sieve. Allow the purée to cool.

Finishing and serving

4 Pour the cooled, strained purée into the *sorbetière* and churn according to the manufacturer's instructions until the sorbet is made. Serve on well-chilled plates or dishes.

Bitter Chocolate Sorbet

Sorbet au chocolat amer

To make 1 litre *(1¾ pints)*

200g *(7 oz)*	unsweetened dark chocolate
500ml *(¾ pint)*	water
300g *(10½ oz)*	sugar
50g *(2 oz)*	sweet dark chocolate

Preparation

1 In a bain-marie, melt the unsweetened chocolate.

2 Measure out the water, which should be lukewarm. Stir it into the melted chocolate and add the sugar.

3   Grate the sweet chocolate finely. Add it to the chocolate already prepared. Allow the mixture to cool.

Finishing

4   Pour the mixture into the *sorbetière* and churn according to the manufacturer's instructions until the sorbet is made.

Serving

5   Serve on well-chilled plates or dishes, accompanied, if you like, by Kumquat Confit (see page 205).

Melon Sorbet

Sorbet au melon

To make 1 litre *(1¾ pints)*

1	large ripe melon, weighing 800g *(1¾ lb)*
180g *(6½ oz)*	sugar
1	lemon

Preparation

1   Remove the seeds and skin of the melon. Weigh out 500g *(1 lb 2 oz)* melon flesh. Squeeze the juice from the lemon.

2   Cut the melon flesh into large cubes. Put them into a liquidiser or food processor with the sugar and lemon juice and reduce everything to a very fine purée.

3   Pass the purée through a *chinois* or conical sieve.

Finishing

4   Pour the sieved mixture into a *sorbetière* and churn it according to the manufacturer's instructions until the sorbet is made.

Hot Desserts

Pancakes Alaska

Crêpes Alaska

For four people

Pancake batter

2	eggs
250ml *(scant ½ pint)*	milk
2 tbsps	oil *or* unsalted butter, melted
	a pinch of salt
125g *(4½ oz)*	plain flour
25g *(1 oz)*	sugar

Sauce

3 tsps	orange zest, finely julienned
200ml *(scant ½ pint)*	orange juice, freshly squeezed
100ml *(scant ¼ pint)*	lemon juice, freshly squeezed
140g *(5 oz)*	sugar

To cook, fill and finish the pancakes

	butter
500ml *(¾ pint)*	vanilla ice-cream (see page 211)
	icing sugar

Preparation

1 To make the pancake batter, simply mix all the ingredients together. It is not necessary to make this batter in advance as it does not need time to stand.

2 For the sauce, put the julienned orange zest, orange juice, lemon juice and sugar into a saucepan. Cook it over a brisk heat for about 5 minutes so that it reduces to no more than 200ml *(a scant ½ pint)*. Remove the pan from the stove and set it aside.

Cooking

3 You need eight very delicate little pancakes. Use two small
non-stick frying pans, 12cm *(4¾ in)* in diameter. Brush
softened butter over the first pan and, without heating it
first, pour in about 2 tablespoonsful of the pancake batter.
Tip the pan this way and that to let the batter completely
cover the base, then, and only then, put the pan over a brisk
heat. Do not turn the pancake until the surface blisters.
Add a tiny piece of butter when you turn the pancake, if
necessary.

Keep the first pancake warm, and make the next one in the
second frying pan; this allows the first pan to cool down. If
it is not cold enough when you come to use it again, run
cold water over the underside. (A cool pan is the secret of
making really thin pancakes. If the pan is hot, the batter
coagulates as soon as it touches it, making the pancakes an
irregular shape and thicker in some places than others.)

Continue cooking until you have made eight pancakes.
Keep them warm.

Finishing and serving

4 Reheat the sauce. Pre-heat the grill.

5 The pancakes should be hot. Put a small tablespoonful of
vanilla ice-cream into each one, then fold it into a slipper
shape.

6 Arrange two 'slippers' on each plate (the plates need to be
somewhat heat-resistant). Powder the slippers with icing
sugar and put them under the grill for 30 seconds.

7 Coat each pair of pancakes with 1 tablespoon of boiling-hot
sauce and serve immediately.

Gratin of Oranges Madame France

Gratin d'oranges Madame France

This recipe is dedicated to a charming old lady from Rheims, who used to come to the restaurant every Sunday for a champagne luncheon. Her friends called her 'Madame France'.

For four people

16	segments of 'oriental oranges' (see page 207)
50g *(2 oz)*	*crème pâtissière* (see page 256)
30g *(1 oz)*	orange jelly marmalade
4 tbsps	juice from the 'oriental oranges'
4 tbsps	double cream
6 tbsps	whipping cream
2 tsps	unsalted pistachio nuts, chopped
	Grand Marnier *or* Curaçao

Preparation

1 Prepare the 'oriental oranges' and the *crème pâtissière* (see pages 207 and 256).

2 Using a whisk, mix the *crème pâtissière*, orange jelly, orange juice and double cream. Whisk well to make it really smooth, with no lumps. Add a drop of Grand Marnier or Curaçao.

3 Whisk the whipping cream to a light foam (like a *crème Chantilly*). Fold it into the previously made mixture.

4 Arrange the orange segments on a little cast-iron egg-dish, about 13–15cm *(5–6 in)* in diameter. Cover them thickly with the creamy mixture.

Finishing and serving

5 Glaze the cream by holding it under a very hot grill or a salamander until the surface is coloured. Sprinkle it with the chopped pistachios and serve immediately.

Little Soufflés of Citrus and Kiwi Fruits

Petit soufflé d'agrumes aux kiwis

For four people

Soufflé mixture

2	egg yolks
4	egg whites
140g *(5 oz)*	caster sugar
1 tbsp	orange juice
	unsalted butter

Sauce

3 tsp	orange zest, finely julienned
	juice of 2 oranges
100g *(3½ oz)*	sugar
1 tbsp	fresh lime juice
½	kiwi fruit

Garnish

2	oranges
1½	kiwi fruits

Preparation

1 To make the sauce, put the orange juice, julienne of orange zest, sugar and lime juice into a saucepan. Cook over a fierce heat for 7–8 minutes, until the liquid becomes very syrupy. Remove the pan from the heat and set it aside.

2 Peel the kiwis and cut each one from top to bottom into twelve sections. Keep sixteen sections for the garnish. Chop the remaining eight coarsely and set them and the sections aside, both covered with transparent film to keep out the air.

3 Peel the two whole oranges down to the flesh and remove the membranes from the segments. Cover the separated segments with transparent film and set them aside.

Finishing

4 Pre-heat the oven to 280°C/530°F/Gas 10. Butter four little soufflé dishes measuring 5cm *(2 in)* in diameter.

5 In a basin, whisk the egg yolks with half the sugar until they become pale and fluffy.

6   In another basin, whisk the egg whites with the rest of the sugar.

7   Fill a baking tin with water (this will serve as a bain-marie for the soufflés). Put the tin on to the stove to heat the water so that it will be boiling when the time comes to cook the soufflés.

8   Add the tablespoon of orange juice to the beaten egg whites, then fold them into the beaten yolks. Fill the little buttered moulds and put them into the bain-marie (with the water boiling) for 3 minutes.

9   Take the moulds out of the bain-marie and slide them into the lowest part of the pre-heated oven. Cook them for exactly 3 minutes.

10 Reheat the sauce while the soufflés cook. Add the reserved chopped kiwi.

Serving

11 Unmould the soufflés on to warm plates. Decorate each plate with four sections of kiwi and six of orange. Coat with the orange sauce and serve without delay.

Passion Fruit Soufflé

Soufflé au fruit de la passion

This is one of the most often-asked-for desserts at Crissier.

For two people

150ml *(¼ pint)*	passion fruit juice (see editor's note, page 204)
1	egg yolk
2	egg whites
70g *(2½ oz)*	sugar
	unsalted butter

Preparation and cooking

1   Pre-heat the oven to 220°C/430°F/Gas 7. Carefully brush the inside of a 12cm- *(4¾in-)* diameter soufflé dish with softened butter.

2 Beat the egg yolk with half the sugar until the mixture becomes pale and fluffy.

3 Whisk the egg whites with half the remaining sugar until they have almost begun to thicken, then add the rest of the sugar and whisk to soft-peak consistency.

4 Add 2 tablespoons of the passion fruit juice to the egg yolk mixture, then delicately but thoroughly incorporate one-third of the beaten egg white. Fold in the remaining two-thirds with a spatula.

5 Fill the buttered soufflé dish with the mixture and bake the soufflé for 10–12 minutes in the pre-heated oven.

Finishing

6 While the soufflé cooks, lightly sweeten the rest of the passion fruit juice and heat it in a bain-marie, just to warm it and no more. Put the sauce into a sauceboat.

Serving

7 Bring the soufflé to the table in its dish with the warm juice in its sauceboat. Divide the soufflé between two plates and surround each helping with half the juice.

Souffléed Cherry Soup

Soupe de cerises soufflée

Cherries are not used nearly enough for desserts, which is a pity.

Editor's note – By 'soup' Fredy Girardet means what we would call a compote.

For four people

Cherry 'soup'

1kg *(2¼ lb)*	black cherries, stoned, weighing 400g *(14 oz)*
30g *(1 oz)*	unsalted butter
60g *(2 oz)*	sugar
	kirsch

Soufflé

1	egg yolk
2	egg whites
70g *(2½ oz)*	sugar
1½ tbsps	lemon juice

Preparation

1 One day in advance, put 400g *(14 oz)* stoned cherries into a frying pan with the butter. Cook them gently until the juice runs. Add the sugar and continue cooking until the sugar slightly caramelises. At this point, pour in a generous dash of kirsch and flambé it. Take the pan off the stove.

2 Put the cherries into a strainer to drain them, and keep the juice.

3 Just before serving, pre-heat the oven to 260°C/500°F/ Gas 10.

4 Divide the cherries between four little soufflé dishes 6cm *(2⅜ in)* in diameter and just cover them with their juice.

5 Prepare the soufflé mixture. Put the egg yolk into a basin with 35g *(1¼ oz)* sugar. Beat it until it becomes pale and fluffy. Add half a tablespoon of lemon juice.

6 In another basin, whisk the egg whites to firm peaks with the rest of the sugar, then fold in a tablespoon of lemon juice. Fold the whites delicately into the yolk mixture using a spatula.

7 Top up the moulds with the soufflé mixture.

Finishing and serving

8 Bake the soufflés at the bottom of the pre-heated oven for 5 minutes. Serve immediately.

Pâtisserie

Wine Tart

Tarte au vin

This is a recipe from the Vaud: both the pastry and the filling are local specialities.

Editor's note – If you cannot get Vaudois wine, use any good dry white wine instead.

For six people

Pastry

140g *(5 oz)*	plain flour
1 tsp	baking powder
60g *(2¼ oz)*	unsalted butter, softened
	a pinch of salt
½ tsp	sugar
3 tbsps	milk
	butter and flour for the tart tin

Filling

120g *(4 oz)*	caster sugar
1 tsp	ground cinnamon
10g *(¼ oz)*	plain flour
100ml *(scant ¼ pint)*	white Vaudois wine
15g *(approx. ½ oz)*	butter

Preparation and cooking

1 Pre-heat the oven to 260°C/500°F/Gas 10. Lightly butter a tart tin with a removable base 20cm *(8 in)* in diameter.

2 To make the pastry, put the flour, baking powder and softened butter together in a large bowl. Add the salt and sugar. Rub all the ingredients together with your fingertips

until the mixture resembles coarse semolina. Add the milk and mix it in lightly and rapidly with your fingers, without exerting any pressure. Form the pastry into a ball, using it to collect all the loose flour. If need be, add another drop or two of milk.

3   Do not let the pastry rest, but roll it out straight away to fit the prepared tart tin. The pastry should be only 3mm (⅛ in) thick and should extend well beyond the rim. Ease the pastry into the base of the tin by pressing gently into the corners with a small ball of dough, but arrange for the spare pastry at the top of the tin to project as a little horizontal fold or lip about 1cm (⅜ in) wide and 1cm (⅜ in) deep inside the tin. There is now much less spare pastry all round the outside of the tin. Press the pastry down on top of the rim with your thumb and trim it off neatly by rolling the pin across the tin.

4   Finish the edge of this tart in the way we finish all our tarts at Crissier – that is, press the fold of pastry inside the tin upwards (the rolling pin should have passed over it without touching it at all). Work fast, with your fingers inside the rim. You now have a border standing up all round the top of the tin, with the lower, outside edge firmly attached to the rim. Pinch this border between your finger and thumb with tweaking movements, at intervals of 1cm (⅜ in) to make a little fluted edge all round the top of the tart.

5   Mix the sugar, cinnamon and flour together. Strew this mixture all over the bottom of the tart. (This is a liquid filling so the bottom of the tart is not pricked with a fork.) Pour the wine over the sugar mixture and mix it in with your fingertips. Dot the surface with the butter, in flakes.

6   Cook the tart in the bottom of the pre-heated oven for 15–20 minutes, turning it from time to time to equalise the heat and to prevent bubbles forming.

7   Leave the tart to cool before taking it out of the tin.

Tart Raisiné

Tarte au raisiné

This is an old Vaudois country recipe. In the autumn, on farms all over the region, the juice of apples and pears is reduced very slowly, for 48 hours, in large cauldrons to make our *raisiné*.

Editor's note – There is no substitute for *raisiné*, which is a thick, dark brown concentrate of fruit juices. It is sold locally in the markets, but not in shops. Either try to buy some in Switzerland or eat this tart when you get there.

For six people

250g *(9 oz)*	sweet flan pastry (see page 255)
	butter and flour for the tart tin

Filling

3	eggs
1	egg yolk
150ml *(¼ pint)*	double cream
100ml *(scant ¼ pint)*	raisiné (see notes above)

Preparation and cooking

1 Make 250g *(9 oz)* sweet flan pastry and leave it to rest in the refrigerator.

2 Pre-heat the oven to 260°C/500°F/Gas 10. Butter and flour a 20cm *(8 in)* tart ring, or a tart tin with a removable base, and line it with the pastry (see page 228, steps 3 and 4). Protect the pastry with a disc of aluminium foil pressed well against the edges and over the rim.

3 Blind-bake the pastry in the pre-heated oven for about 10–15 minutes. Leave it to cool in the tin. Reduce the oven temperature to 180°C/350°F/Gas 4.

4 Prepare the filling by whisking together the eggs, egg yolk, cream and the *raisiné*. (It may be better to increase the quantity of *raisiné* by 1 tablespoon, but this depends on the degree to which it was reduced when it was made.)

5 Partly fill the pastry shell, then put it into the oven and complete the filling by spooning in the rest of the mixture – it must fill the shell to the brim and this way there is no danger of spilling it when you put it in the oven.

6 Leave the oven door ajar until the filling is set; this should take about half an hour. Test its firmness by giving the tart tin a little shake.

7 When the tart is cooked, take it out of the oven. Allow it to cool a little then take it out of the tin and leave it to get quite cold on a cake rack.

Lemon Tart
Tarte au citron

For six people

250g *(9 oz)* sweet flan pastry (see page 255)
butter and flour for the tart tin

Filling
3   eggs
1   egg yolk
juice of 3 lemons
juice of 1 orange
150ml *(¼ pint)* double cream
150g *(5½ oz)* sugar

Preparation and cooking

1 Make 250g *(9 oz)* sweet flan pastry and leave it to rest in the refrigerator.

2 Pre-heat the oven to 260°C/500°F/Gas 10. Butter and lightly flour a 20cm *(8 in)* tart tin with a removable base. Line it with the pastry (see page 228, steps 3 and 4) and blind-bake it for 10–15 minutes in the pre-heated oven. Take care to protect the pastry with a disc of aluminium foil, which should be pressed up to and over the edges before it is weighted down. When it is cooked, let it cool without taking it out of the tin. Lower the oven temperature to 180°C/350°F/Gas 4.

3 Whisk all the ingredients for the tart filling together – the eggs, orange and lemon juice, cream and sugar.

4   When the mixture is nice and frothy, pour most of it into the tart shell. The mixture needs to come right to the top, but to avoid spilling it put the partly filled tart into the oven (with the temperature now reduced) and finish filling it with a spoon.

5   Bake the tart with the oven door ajar, and wait until the filling has become firm. This should take about 35 minutes. Check the firmness of the filling by giving the tin a little shake.

6   Take the tart out of the tin when it is lukewarm and leave it on a cake rack to cool. If you like, decorate it with a few neat segments of peeled lemon.

Raspberry Tart
Tarte aux framboises

It is particularly important not to allow the filling of this tart to boil – it might do so towards the end of its cooking time.

For four people

250g *(9 oz)*	sweet flan pastry (see page 255)
	butter and flour for the tart tin

Filling

200g *(7 oz)*	raspberries, preferably fresh
1	egg
2	egg yolks
70g *(2½ oz)*	sugar
100ml *(scant ¼ pint)*	double cream

Preparation

1   Pre-heat the oven to 260°C/500°F/Gas 10. Lightly butter and flour an 18cm *(7 in)* tart tin with a removable base.

2 Make 250g *(9 oz)* sweet flan pastry. Leave it to rest, then use it to line the prepared tart tin (see page 228, steps 3 and 4). Blind-bake it for about 10–15 minutes in the pre-heated oven, protecting the edges with aluminium foil. Leave it to cool in its tin. Reduce the oven temperature to 190°C/375°F/Gas 5.

Cooking

3 Whisk the egg, egg yolks, sugar and cream together, making sure the sugar dissolves.

4 Arrange the raspberries on the bottom of the pre-cooked pastry shell, pointed ends facing upwards, in concentric circles. Cover them with the egg mixture.

5 Bake the tart for about 40 minutes in the bottom of the oven, at its now reduced temperature. Watch very carefully to see that the filling never reaches boiling point.

6 When the tart has cooled completely, take it out of the tin.

Tart Vaudoise with Cream
Tarte vaudoise à la crème

The secret of this marvellous tart was given to me by a local grandmother. Both the pastry and the filling are Vaudois specialities.

For eight people

Pastry

140g *(5 oz)*	plain flour
1 tsp	baking powder
60g *(2¼ oz)*	unsalted butter, softened
	a pinch of salt
½ tsp	sugar
3 tbsps	milk
	butter and flour for the tart tin

Filling

100g *(3½ oz)*	sugar
	a good pinch of plain flour
250ml *(scant ½ pint)*	double cream
	powdered cinnamon
	unsalted butter

Preparation and cooking

1 Pre-heat the oven to 260°C/500°F/Gas 10. Lightly butter and flour a 25cm *(10 in)* tart tin with sloping sides and no rim.

2 Make the pastry and line the tin (see page 228, steps 2, 3 and 4).

3 Mix the sugar with the pinch of flour. Sprinkle it all over the bottom of the pastry case and shake the tin so that the sugar settles evenly.

4 Pour the cream on top of the sugar and mix it in a little with your fingertips so that it is distributed evenly over the whole surface of the tart.

5 Sprinkle the cream with a light dusting of cinnamon. Put a few flakes of butter on top and bake the tart in the pre-heated oven for a good half an hour. The cream should thicken and darken, but do not let it burn.

6 Slide it out of the tin while it is still warm. Leave it to cool completely on a cake rack.

Almond and Honey Cakes
Galettes au miel

This is a very practical recipe and is good for keeping.

For six to eight people

250g *(9 oz)*	sweet flan pastry (see page 255)
20g *(¾ oz)*	apricot jelly, for glazing

Filling

125g *(4½ oz)*	sugar
125g *(4½ oz)*	slivered almonds
90g *(3¼ oz)*	unsalted butter
35g *(1¼ oz)*	honey
2 tbsps	double cream
50g *(2 oz)*	crystallised fruits, chopped
	kirsch

Preparation

1 Pre-heat the oven to 200°C/400°F/Gas 6. Grease a tart tin with a removable base 22cm *(8½ in)* in diameter.

2 Roll out the pastry to fit the tart tin. Line the tin with the pastry (see page 228, steps 3 and 4) and prick the bottom all over with a fork. Bake it for 10 minutes at the bottom of the pre-heated oven. Leave the pastry shell in the tin.

Cooking

3 Lightly brush a thin layer of apricot glaze over the bottom of the pastry shell.

4 Put all the ingredients for the filling into a saucepan and heat them gently, stirring to mix them well as they melt.

5 Raise the oven to 210°C/410°F/Gas 6½. When the filling is melted, spread it in a thin layer on the glazed pastry shell. Cook it for about 15 minutes in the pre-heated oven. It is ready when the filling begins to bubble.

6 Leave the cake to cool in its tin, then take it out.

Serving

7 Cut the cake into little triangles or rectangular pieces. Serve them with coffee, like *petits fours.*

Macaroon Cake
Gâteau sec aux noisettes

Editor's note – As the pastry base of this cake needs to be very thin, you can use leftover flaky pastry scraps.

For six people

100g *(3½ oz)*	flaky pastry (see page 253)
30g *(1 oz)*	raspberries (fresh or frozen)
110g *(3¾ oz)*	sugar
75g *(2½ oz)*	ground hazelnuts
2	egg whites
	grated rind of 1 lemon
	caster sugar
	icing sugar
	slivered almonds

Preparation

1 Purée the raspberries in a liquidiser with 35g *(1¼ oz)* of the sugar, then, unless you do not object to the little raspberry pips getting in your teeth, pass the mixture through a *tamis.*

2 Prepare a macaroon paste by mixing, with a spatula, the rest of the sugar, the ground powdered nuts, the egg whites and lemon rind.

3 Roll out the pastry to a thickness of 2–3mm *(⅛ in)* and line an 18cm *(7 in)* tart tin with a removable base. Prick it all over with the prongs of a fork. (Put it in a refrigerator if you are not going to bake it at once.)

Cooking and finishing

4 Pre-heat the oven to 220°C/425°F/Gas 7.

5 Lightly sprinkle caster sugar over the uncooked pastry, then spread the raspberry purée over it in a smooth layer.

6 Spread the macaroon mixture over the raspberry, smoothing the surface with the help of a spatula.

7 Cook the cake for 40 minutes in the pre-heated oven. Reduce the heat to 180°C/350°F/Gas 4 after 20 minutes if it is browning too quickly. Take it out and leave it to cool a little.

8 Scatter the slivered almonds over the top of the cake while it is still warm. Sprinkle the cake with icing sugar then put it under a hot grill for just long enough to caramelise the sugar lightly. Take care, as this takes barely a minute.

9 Let the cake cool, then take it out of the tin.

Strawberry Mille-feuille
Mille-feuille aux fraises

In winter, we use pineapple instead of strawberries and kirsch instead of raspberry liqueur.

For six people

100g *(3½ oz)*	strawberries, stems removed
250g *(9 oz)*	flaky pastry (see page 253)
1	egg yolk, for glazing
	icing sugar
200ml *(scant ½ pint)*	whipping cream
60g *(2¼ oz)*	sugar
2 tbsps	*crème pâtissière* (see page 256)
1 tbsp	raspberry liqueur

Preparation and cooking

1 Pre-heat the oven to 260°C/500°F/Gas 10.

2 Roll out the flaky pasty in a 30cm *(12 in)* square, 2mm *(⅛ in)* thick. Put it on to a baking sheet and prick the surface with a fork.

3 Prepare the glaze by beating the egg yolk with a little water. Brush it all over the surface of the pastry, taking care not to let it run down the sides.

4   Bake the pastry in the pre-heated oven for 35 minutes, looking at it from time to time. But do not under-cook it – one of the secrets of a successful *mille-feuille* is to have it very well cooked and quite dry.

5   Take the pastry out of the oven when it is well risen and done. Leave it on its baking sheet. Sprinkle it with icing sugar and put it under a hot grill for a few seconds to caramelise it. Leave it to cool.

6   Trim the edges of the pastry and cut it into three equally wide slices. Turn them over, sprinkle them with icing sugar and again put them under the grill to caramelise them. Leave them to cool.

7   Cut the strawberries into 1cm *(⅜ in)* dice.

Finishing

8   Whip the cream *en Chantilly.* Whisk in the sugar, *crème pâtissière* and a small tablespoonful of the raspberry liqueur.

9   Put the first slice of *mille-feuille* on to a little board. Coat its top with a base 1cm *(⅜ in)* of the cream. Cover this with half the diced strawberries, then cover them with more cream, but this layer of strawberries and cream should not be thicker than a good 1cm *(approx. ½ in)*.

10   Put the second slice of *mille-feuille* on top of the first and cover it with cream, strawberries and more cream, exactly like the first slice.

11   Cover the second slice with the third slice and spread the sides of the cake with more cream, evening it out with a spatula.

Fanny's Tea-time Sponge Cake

Biscuit pour le thé de Fanny

This cake, which is excellent for afternoon tea, is best made the day before.

For eight people

3	eggs
150g *(5½ oz)*	sugar
	a pinch of salt
100g *(3½ oz)*	unsalted butter, softened
	grated rind of 1 lemon
300g *(10½ oz)*	plain flour
150ml *(¼ pint)*	milk
100ml *(scant ¼ pint)*	double cream
3 tsps	baking powder
	butter for the cake tin

Preparation and cooking

1 Pre-heat the oven to 220°C/425°F/Gas 7. Butter a cake tin 30cm *(12 in)* long and 10cm *(4 in)* wide.

2 Mix the eggs and sugar. Add the pinch of salt and whisk until the mixture becomes light and frothy.

3 Add the butter, grated lemon rind and flour. Mix energetically with a spatula until you have a smooth dough.

4 Finally, incorporate the milk, cream and baking powder. Beat everything in carefully with the spatula.

5 Pour the mixture into the buttered cake tin. Tap it on the table to level the surface and get rid of any bubbles.

6 Bake the cake in the pre-heated oven for 45 minutes.

Wild Strawberry Sandwich Sponge Cake

Génoise aux fraises des bois

If you have no wild strawberries, use any other soft red fruits.

For six people

1	génoise sponge cake, cooked the day before (see page 256)
300g *(10½ oz)*	wild strawberries
50g *(2 oz)*	sugar
	strawberry *or* raspberry liqueur
200g *(7 oz)*	slivered almonds
400ml *(⅔ pint)*	whipping cream
200g *(7 oz)*	royal icing (see page 258)

Preparation

1 Make a little light syrup with 25g *(1 oz)* sugar, 3 tablespoons of warm water and a few drops of strawberry or raspberry liqueur.

2 Toast the slivered almonds in a warm oven, heated to 180°C/350°F/Gas 4. Put them on to a dry baking sheet and turn them from time to time to give them an even colour.

3 Using a long saw-edged or scalloped knife, cut the sponge cake into three equally thick horizontal slices.

4 Whip the cream with the rest of the sugar to make a *Chantilly*. Reserve 3–4 tablespoons to coat the side of the cake.

5 Lay the three slices of cake on the table and lightly soak them with the syrup. Brush it on to the slices with a pastry brush.

Finishing

6 Divide the strawberries into three equal parts: two will be used in the 'sandwich'; the third will decorate the top of the cake, so reserve the best berries for that. Spread half the whipped cream on the first slice of cake, then distribute the first batch of strawberries on top.

7 Put the second slice on top of the first. Cover it with the rest of the cream and the second lot of strawberries.

8 Put the third slice on top of the second slice. With a spatula, smooth off the cream that may be oozing out at the sides and make sure the surface is level.

9 Prepare 200g *(7 oz)* royal icing.

10 Pour the icing over the top of the cake and let it spread out of its own accord, then even it out with a spatula dipped in hot water. Take care not to touch the sponge, as you need to keep the surface white.

11 Cover the sides of the cake with a little *Chantilly* cream. Decorate them with the toasted almond slivers.

12 Decorate the top of the cake with a circle of the remaining strawberries. Serve the cake well chilled.

Basic Preparations

Chicken Stock

Fond de volaille

All stocks can be kept in the freezer. For home use, make 1 litre
(1¾ pints) at a time.

Editor's note – Freeze these stocks in small quantities. They will be
more useful like this; otherwise you may have to thaw more than
you need at one time.

To make 2.5 litres *(just over 4 pints)*

1	chicken
	several chicken giblets
1	onion, studded with a clove
1	leek
1	stick of celery
1	clove of garlic, crushed
100g *(3½ oz)*	carrots
1	bouquet garni
4 litres *(7 pints)*	water
	salt

Preparation and cooking

1 Wash, peel (if necessary) and coarsely chop all the
   vegetables.

2 At the same time, start cooking the chicken and giblets in
   cold unsalted water. Bring to the boil and add the
   vegetables. Continue cooking for 4 hours, skimming
   frequently.

3 Carefully remove the chicken. The meat can be used as a
   stuffing for vegetables, croquettes, etc.

4 Strain the stock through a sieve in which you have laid a
   dampened muslin cloth or a layer of dampened, wrung-out
   cotton-wool. Season very lightly with salt and let it cool.

White Stock

Fond blanc

To make about 1.5 litres *(2½ pints)*

1	shin of veal, sawn in pieces
½	calf's foot, chopped into pieces
2	chicken carcasses, broken up
2	onions, each studded with a clove
2	carrots
1	leek
½	celeriac root
1	bouquet garni (thyme, parsley, bay leaf)
1 level tsp	black peppercorns, coarsely crushed *(mignonnette)* (see editor's note, page 7)

Preparation and cooking

1 Soak all the bones in cold water for 1 hour, then blanch them.

2 Put the bones into a large saucepan. Cover them generously with cold water and bring them slowly to the boil, skimming frequently.

3 When the skimming is completed, and with the water boiling gently, add the vegetables, the bouquet garni and the crushed peppercorns. Cook gently, uncovered, for 4 hours, skimming from time to time.

4 Strain the stock through a sieve.

5 Return the stock to a clean pan and continue to cook it over a high heat. You need to reduce it so that it forms a light jelly when cold. It is ready when a thin layer spread on a saucer solidifies in 2 minutes in the freezer.

6 To make a *fond brun* (brown stock) use the same ingredients as above, but instead of blanching the bones as in step 1, roast them in a very hot oven until they are a good dark brown, then proceed as for white stock, steps 2–5.

Fish Stock

Fond de poisson

To make 500ml *(a scant pint)*

1kg *(1 lb 2 oz)*	sole and turbot bones
500ml *(a scant pint)*	dry white wine
500ml *(a scant pint)*	water
1	onion, studded with a clove
1	bouquet of vegetables (leek, carrot, celery, parsley)
1	bay leaf

Preparation and cooking

1 Soak the bones well under running cold water, turning frequently for 1 hour. Break them into pieces.

2 Put the pieces in a saucepan with the white wine and water. Bring slowly to the boil, then reduce to a simmer and skim frequently.

3 When the skimming is completed, add the vegetables and the bay leaf and cook gently for 30–35 minutes.

4 Strain the stock, then return it to a clean pan and continue to reduce it by a little or a lot, depending on the recipe for which it is intended.

Vegetable Stock

Bouillon de légumes

I use this stock more often than fish stock. It is particularly good for sauces enriched with butter, as its taste is more subtle.

To make 1 litre *(1¾ pints)*

1 litre *(1¾ pints)*	water
1 litre *(1¾ pints)*	dry white wine
2	tomatoes
1	leek
1	large carrot
½	celeriac root ⟩ coarsely chopped
1	large onion
2	shallots
6	cloves of garlic, cut in two
1	bouquet garni (parsley, thyme, bay leaf, clove)
	a little sea salt
	black peppercorns, coarsely crushed *(mignonnettes)* (see editor's note, page 7)

Preparation and cooking

1   Put all the ingredients in a large saucepan, taking care not to add too much salt. Bring it to the boil, then leave it, uncovered, to simmer slowly for 3 hours, stirring from time to time.

2   Strain the stock through a sieve. The liquid will have reduced by half.

Use this stock for certain reductions, to add to sauces that have been reduced too much, for white butter sauce *(beurre blanc)*, to rescue a *beurre blanc* that has gone wrong, or for certain braised fish recipes.

Veal Stock and Veal Glaze

Fond de veau et glace de veau

If you like, you can add 1 tablespoon of concentrated tomato purée to the bones in step 1.

To make 1.5 litres *(2½ pints)*

1kg *(1 lb 2 oz)*	veal bones, chopped
100g *(3½ oz)*	carrots
100g (3½ oz)	onions
1	leek
1	shallot
1	clove of garlic
1	bouquet garni (thyme, parsley, bay leaf)

Preparation and cooking

1 Heat the oven to 260°C/500°F/Gas 10. Put the bones into a roasting pan in the oven to become a good dark brown.

2 Peel and coarsely chop the vegetables. Add them to the roasting pan when the bones are already half browned.

3 Put the browned bones and vegetables into a large saucepan with the garlic and bouquet garni. Add enough water to cover the bones generously. Bring slowly to the boil, skimming whenever fat forms.

4 Continue cooking, uncovered, at a gentle simmer for 4 hours. Skim when necessary and, if need be, add a little water during cooking so that the bones remain covered.

5 Strain the stock.

Veal glaze

6 After the stock has been strained, reduce it until less than one-third remains – 1 litre *(1¾ pints)* of stock, for example, should be reduced to 300ml *(½ pint)* of glaze.

Game Stock

Fond de gibier

To make 500ml *(a scant pint)*

750g *(1½ lb)*	carcasses, giblets and other scraps of game
	oil
300g *(10½ oz)*	mirepoix (see page 251)
1 liqueur-glass	cognac
500ml *(a scant pint)*	red *or* white wine
1.5 litres *(2½ pints)*	veal stock (see page 247)

Preparation and cooking

1   Heat the oven to 260°C/500°F/Gas 10. Put all the game carcasses, giblets and scraps into a roasting pan with a little oil and leave them to become a good dark brown.

2   Make the mirepoix and leave it in its saucepan. Heat it up and deglaze the mixture into the cognac, then ignite it.

3   Remove the roasting pan from the oven when the bones are brown and deglaze with the wine. (The colour of the wine depends on the recipe for which the stock is intended.)

4   Put the flambéed mirepoix, with the bones and wine, into a large saucepan. Add the veal stock. Bring it to a simmer, then leave it to cook very gently for 4 hours, skimming frequently. If need be, add a little water during this cooking time, as the bones and meat must be kept just covered.

5   Strain the stock into a basin and leave it to cool, so that the fat comes to the surface. Remove the fat.

6   Put the stock, freed of fat, back into a clean pan. Reduce it until it thickens slightly and there is no more than 500ml *(a scant pint)* left. To test the reduction, ladle a tiny amount on to a cold plate; it should set at once.

Aspic of Meat, Game or Poultry

Gelée de viande, volaille ou gibier

To make 1 litre *(1¾ pints)*

1	shin-bone of veal, with 200g *(7 oz)* meat, chopped into pieces, *or* trimmings of game or chicken (see variations below)
2	calves' feet, chopped
1	bouquet garni (thyme, parsley, bay leaf, carrot, leek)
2 litres *(3½ pints)*	water
1	carrot ⎫
1	medium-sized onion ⎬ cut into 5mm *(¼ in)* dice
½	white part of a leek ⎭
1	sprig of tarragon, chopped
1	egg white
	oil
	salt and pepper

Preparation and cooking

1 Mince the veal and set it aside.

2 Lightly fry the bones (or trimmings of game and poultry) and the pieces of calves' feet in a large saucepan with a little oil.

3 Add the bouquet garni and 2 litres *(3½ pints)* water, then simmer the stock for about 12 hours. The water should barely tremble. Add fresh water from time to time to keep it at the same level.

4 At the end of its cooking time, strain the stock through a fine sieve.

5 Prepare the ingredients for clarifying the stock, mixing together the minced veal, diced vegetables, tarragon, egg white and, if necessary, a little water, so that they form a compact but moist mixture.

6 Add the meat-and-vegetable mixture to the strained stock. Put it on the stove in a saucepan, bring it slowly to the boil, then lower the heat and leave it to simmer gently for at least 20 minutes.

7 Strain the stock through a piece of dampened muslin placed at the bottom of a fine sieve or *chinois*. Season to taste. Keep the aspic in a cool place.

Variations

To make a game aspic, substitute the shin of veal with 1kg *(2¼ lb)* venison trimmings, browning them first, as in step 2 above.

To make a chicken aspic, substitute the shin of veal with a chicken. It is not browned first, however, but is merely cooked in the water, as in step 3 above.

Crayfish Butter

Beurre d'écrevisses

Instead of crayfish carcasses you could use the carcasses of four lobsters or the shells of twelve *langoustines* (Dublin Bay prawns). The quantities of vegetables and butter remain the same.

32	crayfish carcasses
1	head of garlic
1	onion
20g *(¾ oz)*	celery
	olive oil
100g *(3½ oz)*	unsalted butter
100ml *(¼ pint)*	dry white wine
3	sprigs of parsley
2	sprigs of thyme
1	sprig of rosemary

Preparation and cooking

1 Cut the head of garlic and the onion in two horizontally. Chop the celery coarsely and brown garlic, onion and celery in some olive oil in a heavy saucepan.

2 Put the crayfish carcasses with the butter into a food processor and work them to a fine mush.

3 Add the crayfish mixture to the vegetables, cook and stir well to prevent sticking. Let all the juices reduce and turn brown. Continue cooking, stirring occasionally, until a skin forms over the bottom of the saucepan.

4 Add the white wine and then add water to come to the top of the crayfish mixture – or, even better (and if you have kept it), top up with the water in which the crayfish were cooked. Add the parsley, thyme and rosemary, and cook for half an hour.

5 Strain the mixture through a *chinois*, pressing it well to extract all the liquid.

Finishing

6 Leave the strained liquid to cool, then skim off the fat that has solidified on top; this forms the crayfish butter.

Mirepoix

Mirepoix

To make six tablespoons

2 tbsp carrot ⎫
2 tbsp onion ⎬ chopped into 5mm *(¼ in)* dice
2 tbsp leek ⎭
       a little shallot
       bouquet garni
       unsalted butter

Preparation

1 Cook the ingredients gently in a little butter for 3–4 minutes. As soon as the vegetables have sweated a little, discard the bouquet garni and use the mirepoix according to the instructions in the recipe you are following.

2 Garlic can be added if the recipe is suitable – as it would be, for instance, with lamb.

Sauce Poivrade

Sauce poivrade

By adding cream to this recipe you can make Sauce Grand Veneur.

For four people

6 tbsps	mirepoix (see page 251)
4	cloves of garlic, unpeeled
1 tsp	coarsely crushed black peppercorns *(mignonnette)*
1 liqueur-glass	cognac
1 tbsp	vinegar
300ml *(just over ½ pint)*	game stock (see page 248)
50g *(2 oz)*	unsalted butter
	salt and pepper

Preparation and cooking

1   Make the mirepoix, adding the garlic and black pepper.

2   As soon as the mirepoix is ready, add the cognac, heat it and ignite it. Cook until it is completely reduced.

3   Add the vinegar and stock and leave it to simmer, uncovered, for about an hour.

4   Strain the sauce. You should have about 100ml *(a scant ¼ pint)* of liquid left. This is the *poivrade* base.

Finishing

5   Season this basic sauce and add to it any juices that have run from the game that the sauce is to accompany.

6   Enrich the sauce by gradually whisking in the cold, diced butter. Taste for seasoning: pepper should predominate.

Ravioli Dough
Pâte à ravioli

This dough will not keep long without drying out.

To make about 400g *(14 oz)*

250g *(9 oz)*	plain flour
3	small eggs, weighing 150g *(6 oz)*
	a pinch of salt
	a pinch of grated nutmeg

Preparation

1   Put the flour, a pinch of salt and 1 egg into a food processor. Add a little grated nutmeg and work the machine on slow speed, using the pasta blades.

2   As soon as the first egg is absorbed, add the second, then the third. Work slowly at first, then faster, until the dough forms itself into a firm but elastic and non-sticky ball.

3   Wrap the ball of dough in plastic film and leave it in the refrigerator for at least half an hour before rolling it out.

Flaky Pastry
Pâte feuilletée

Temperature is crucial for this pastry: it must be made in a very, very cool place.

To make 2kg *(4½ lb)*

Basic dough (la détrempe)

1kg *(2¼ lb)*	plain flour
200g *(7 oz)*	unsalted butter
22g *(¾ oz)*	salt
350ml *(just over ½ pint)*	iced water

Pastry

1kg *(2¼ lb)*	unsalted butter

Preparation

1 To make the *détrempe*, three hours in advance, knead the flour, the 200g *(7 oz)* butter and the salt in an electric mixer or food processor for 5 minutes, then add the iced water little by little, kneading for 15 minutes.

2 Wrap the *détrempe* in a damp cloth and leave it in the refrigerator for at least 3 hours.

3 To make the flaky pastry, roll out the *détrempe* to make a rectangle 75cm *(30 in)* long and 45.5cm *(18 in)* wide.

4 Cut the 1kg *(2¼ lb)* butter into 3mm *(⅛ in)* slices and cover the *détrempe* with them, leaving an uncovered border 1cm *(⅜ in)* wide all round. Fold this border over the butter, all round.

5 With the long side of the rectangle towards you, divide the dough mentally into three and fold the left-hand third over the middle third. Next, fold the right-hand third over what was the middle section, aligning the edge neatly along the fold you first made between the left and middle sections.

You now have an elongated rectangle consisting of three layers of dough, with the short side (25cm/ *10 in*) facing you and the key *(clé)* of open edges on the left. You must always turn the dough and fold it so that this *clé* finishes on the left.

6 Now turn the *clé* towards you, and roll the pastry to make a square 45cm *(18 in)* wide.

7 Turn the sheet of dough so that the *clé* is once again on the left and roll it out until it is 1m *(39 in)* long. Straighten the edges with a ruler.

8 Turn the *clé* towards you again and give it a double-turn. To do this, mentally draw a line towards you down the middle of the sheet, then fold the left-hand section over to this median line; fold the right-hand section likewise. Then fold the whole thing in half, right side over left, so that the *clé* is once again on your left.

Press one finger into a corner of the dough to show that it has had one double turn and leave it to rest for three-quarters of an hour in the refrigerator, at 3°C/37°F. (Once again it measures 25 × 45cm *(10 × 18 in)*.

9 Repeat steps 7 and 8. You have now given the dough a second double-turn. Mark the corner with two fingertips and put it back into the refrigerator for another three-quarters of an hour.

10 Repeat the same operation twice more, always giving the pastry time to rest. You will have given it four double-turns in all. It is now ready: leave it in the refrigerator until the last moment before using it.

Sweet Flan Pastry

Pâte sucrée

This pastry will keep very well in the refrigerator for a few days, wrapped in transparent film.

Editor's note – Before putting this pastry away, divide it into four to give the most useful amounts for the recipes in this book.

To make 1kg *(2¼ lb)*

300g *(10½ oz)* unsalted butter
500g *(1 lb 2 oz)* plain flour
150g *(5½ oz)* sugar
            a pinch of salt
1   egg yolk
1   egg

Preparation

1 Put the butter, cut into pieces, with the flour, sugar and salt, into a food processor or mixer. Work it until the mixture resembles coarse semolina.

2 Add the egg yolk and the whole egg and do not work the machine for a moment longer than necessary to amalgamate the eggs with the flour mixture. Form it into a ball and leave it to rest in the refrigerator for several hours before using it.

Pastry Cream
Crème pâtissière

To make about 750ml *(1¼ pints)*

2	eggs
3	egg yolks
160g *(6 oz)*	sugar
40g *(1½ oz)*	plain flour
400ml *(⅔ pint)*	milk
½	vanilla pod

Preparation and cooking

1 Whip the whole eggs, egg yolks, sugar and flour together in a basin, then whisk the mixture until it becomes very pale and frothy. This stage will proceed more quickly if you start with the basin in a bain-marie that is not too hot.

2 Place the vanilla pod in the milk and bring it to the boil.

3 Pour the boiling milk on to the whipped eggs, whisking as you do so.

4 Put the mixture back into a saucepan and bring it just to the boil. Take it off the heat and strain it through a sieve. Allow the pastry cream to cool completely before using it.

Génoise Sponge Cake
Génoise

For six people

3	eggs
75g *(2½ oz)*	sugar
75g *(2½ oz)*	plain flour
	a pinch of salt

1 Pre-heat the oven to 210°C/410°F/Gas 6½. Cut a circle of greaseproof paper to fit the bottom of a sponge tin 20cm *(8 in)* in diameter and 6cm *(2½ in)* deep.

2 Break the eggs into a basin. Add the sugar and put the basin into a bain-marie over a gentle heat. Using electric beaters, whisk until the mixture begins to froth and thicken. (This is a lengthy job, which can take a good quarter of an hour, but it is helpful if the mixture is slightly warmed at the beginning. Although the temperature must never rise above 40°C/100°F, the thickening will then proceed a little faster.)

As soon as the mixture begins to froth and thicken, take it out of the bain-marie and continue whisking until it reaches the ribbon stage *(ruban)*.

3 Using a spatula, fold the flour into the mixture with a pinch of salt. Add the flour little by little, keeping the mixture as light as you can.

4 Fill the prepared cake tin with the sponge mixture.

5 Bake the sponge in the pre-heated oven for about 25–35 minutes, giving the tin a quarter-turn two or three times to make sure the heat is evenly distributed.

Uses
Make this cake the day before you need it, then use it for génoise with fresh fruit (see page 239).

Chocolate Génoise
Génoise brune

For six people

70g *(2½ oz)*	plain flour
	a pinch of salt
10g *(¼ oz)*	cocoa powder
40g *(1¼ oz)*	ground almonds
3	eggs
75g *(2½ oz)*	sugar

Preparation and cooking

1 Pre-heat the oven to 210°C/410°F/Gas 6½. Cut a circle of greaseproof paper to fit the bottom of a cake tin 20cm *(8 in)* in diameter and 6cm *(2½ in)* deep.

2　Mix together the flour, salt, cocoa and ground almonds.

3　Whisk the eggs and sugar (see page 257, step 2).

4　Next, fold in the flour-and-cocoa mixture with a spatula. Add it little by little, working carefully to keep the mixture light and airy.

5　Fill the prepared cake tin and bake the sponge for about 35 minutes, turning the tin three or four times during cooking to distribute the heat evenly.

Uses

Make this cake the day before you need it. Use it as a base for cakes such as Black Forest Cake.

Royal Icing

Glace royale

180g *(7 oz)*	icing sugar	
½	egg white	
	lemon juice	

Preparation

1　Mix the icing sugar with the egg white, using a spatula.

2　Add a little lemon juice.

3　If the mixture is too runny, add more icing sugar.

Praline

Pralin

400g *(15 oz)* lump sugar
150g *(5½ oz)* whole almonds, with skins
150g *(5½ oz)* whole hazelnuts, with skins
oil, for the baking sheet

Preparation and cooking

1 Melt the sugar, very gently, in a saucepan. Do not stir until it begins to melt.

2 Once the sugar has liquified and is a good colour, incorporate as many almonds and hazelnuts as it can absorb. Work quickly.

3 Turn the praline on to an oiled baking sheet, 25cm *(9½ in)* in circumference, and leave it to harden.

4 To use the praline, break one or two pieces off as you need them and chop them with a knife before adding them, as necessary, to the recipe you are following. Keep the praline away from damp in an air-tight container.

Index

salsify: roast duck with
salsify, 131–2
sautéed salsifies, 197–8
salt, 8
sauces: butter in, 5
citronnette, 103–4
cream of watercress,
127–8
mousseline, 75–6
orange (sweet), 220–1
oyster, 55–6
Pinot, 138–40
pistou, 84–5
port and caper, 158–9
red wine, 75–6, 90–1,
161–2
sauce Grand Veneur, 252
sauce Poivrade, 252
tomato, 73–4, 84–5
saumon au pistou, 84–5
*saumon en papillote au
citron vert*, 86–7
scallops: feuilleté of
scallops with two
purées, 109–10
grilled scallops and
langoustines with
asparagus, 102–3
langoustines, scallops
and lobster with black
and pink pepper,
114–15
mousse of scallops with
citronnette sauce,
103–4
papillote of scallops and
langoustines with
coriander, 105–6
scallops with chicory
and lime, 107–8
vegetable soup with little
shellfish, 22–3
sea bass: fillets of sea bass
with artichokes, 76–7
fillets of sea bass with
oysters, 78–9
seasoning, 7–8
*selle d'agneau à la graine de
moutarde*, 157–8
shellfish, 97–117
sieves, 10
sole: fillets of sole with
leeks and a red wine
sauce, 90–1
paupiettes of sole and
salmon with saffron,
83–4
sorbet à la pomme, 213
sorbet au chocolat amer,
213–14
sorbet au melon, 214
sorbets: apple, 213
bitter chocolate, 213–14
melon, 214
three citrus fruit, 212

see also ice-cream
soufflé au fruit de la passion,
221–2
soufflés: little soufflés of
citrus and kiwi fruits,
220–1
passion fruit soufflé,
221–2
soufléed cherry soup, 223–4
soupe de cerises soufflée,
223–4
*soupe de légumes aux petits
coquillages*, 22–3
*soupe tiède de moules aux
carottes nouvelles et à
l'aneth*, 20–2
soups: bouillon of crayfish
with dill and caviare,
15–16
cream of asparagus soup
with morels, 26–7
cream of parsley soup with
a fricassée of frogs'
legs, 24–5
cream of tomato soup with
basil, 27–8
cream of wild mushroom
soup with chervil,
29–30
minestrone with crayfish,
17–18
potato soup with mussels
and leeks, 19–20
vegetable soup with little
shellfish, 22–3
warm mussel and carrot
soup with dill, 20–2
spätzli, 198–9
spring onion, 9
spring salad of quail with
duck foie gras, 46–7
stock: chicken, 243
brown, 244
fish, 245
game, 248
veal, 247
vegetable, 246
white, 244
strawberry: strawberry
mille-feuille, 236–7
wild strawberry mousse,
208–9
wild strawberry sandwich
sponge cake, 239–40
*suprême de loup au céleri-
rave et au vinaigre*, 79–80
sweet flan pastry, 255
sweetbreads: boned stuffed
pigeons St Francis,
135–7
salad of sweetbreads and
mangetout peas, 48–9
veal sweetbreads with port
and caper sauce, 158–9
Swiss chard, 184

sautéed fillet of veal
with Swiss chard, 152–3

tarragon: grilled fillets of
dace or trout with
tarragon, 93–4
tarte au raisiné, 229–30
tarte à l'oignon, 68–9
tarte au citron, 230–1
tarte au vin, 227–8
tarte aux framboises, 231–2
tarte Vaudoise á la crème,
232–3
tarts: lemon tart, 230–1
onion tart, 68–9
raspberry tart, 231–2
tart raisiné, 229–30
tart Vaudoise with cream,
232–3
wine tart, 227–8
*terrine de foie gras de
canard*, 35–6
*terrine de poissons du
Léman à la ciboulette*, 33–4
*terrine de primeurs au foie
gras*, 38–40
terrines: jellied chicken,
36–7
terrine of foie gras of
duck, 35–6
terrine of freshwater fish
with chives, 33–4
terrine of spring
vegetables with foie
gras, 38–40
three citrus fruit sorbets, 212
tomato: chicken fricassée
with cucumbers and
tomato, 123–4
cream of tomato soup with
basil, 27–8
fillet of dace with lemon,
capers and tomato,
95–6
salmon with pistou and a
tomato sauce, 84–5
sauce, 73–4

*Les trois sorbets aux
agrumes*, 212
trout: grilled fillets of
trout with tarragon,
93–4
terrine of freshwater fish
with chives, 33–4
truffle juice, 8
truffles, 8
asparagus and fresh truffles
in flaky pastry, 65–7
boned stuffed pigeons
St Francis, 135–7
chicken breasts with leeks
and truffles, 121–2
little ravioli with
truffles, 63–4

265